M000209924

BRAINTEASERS FOR BROADWAY GENIUSES

GENIUSES

500 PUZZLERS TO PERPLEX EVEN THE BIGGEST FANS

PETER FILICHIA

Foreword by Richard Maltby Jr.

APPLAUSE
THEATRE & CINEMA BOOKS
Essex, Connecticut

APPLAUSE
THEATRE & CINEMA BOOKS

An imprint of Globe Pequot, the trade division of
The Rowman & Littlefield Publishing Group, Inc.
4501 Forbes Blvd., Ste. 200
Lanham, MD 20706
www.rowman.com

Distributed by NATIONAL BOOK NETWORK

Copyright © 2023 by Peter Filichia

All rights reserved. No part of this book may be reproduced in any form
or by any electronic or mechanical means, including information storage
and retrieval systems, without written permission from the publisher,
except by a reviewer who may quote passages in a review.

Library of Congress Cataloging-in-Publication Data

Names: Filichia, Peter, author. | Maltby, Richard, Jr., 1937- author of
  foreword.
Title: Brainteasers for Broadway geniuses : (or questions that will send
  you to the internet) / Peter Filichia ; foreword by Richard Maltby, Jr.
Other titles: Questions that will send you to the internet
Description: Essex, Connecticut : Applause, [2023] | Includes
  bibliographical references.
Identifiers: LCCN 2023001694 (print) | LCCN 2023001695 (ebook) |
  ISBN 9781493074952 (paperback) | ISBN 9781493074969 (epub)
Subjects: LCSH: Theater—New York (State)—New York—Miscellanea. |
  Broadway (New York, N.Y.)—Miscellanea.
Classification: LCC PN2277.N5 .F55 2023 (print) | LCC PN2277.N5
  (ebook) | DDC 792.09747/1—dc23/eng/20230410
LC record available at https://lccn.loc.gov/2023001694
LC ebook record available at https://lccn.loc.gov/2023001695

∞™ The paper used in this publication meets the minimum requirements
of American National Standard for Information Sciences—Permanence of
Paper for Printed Library Materials, ANSI/NISO Z39.48-1992

CONTENTS

FOREWORD

There seems to be some natural connection between musicals and games. Perhaps it is because plays are the solitary vision of, usually, one writer, while musicals are composites, the collective construction of many different creators. Assembling all the pieces that compose a musical is not at all unlike doing a jigsaw puzzle, including the attendant fun of the final picture slowly revealing itself as the collective elements begin to come together.

That may also be why musicals seem to attract people who have a certain kind of gaming brain. Stephen Sondheim famously had a townhouse in New York decorated wall-to-wall with antique games, and during the creation of *West Side Story*, Sondheim and Leonard Bernstein used to sit in the empty theater doing cryptic crossword puzzles from the *London Times*—competitively, to see who could finish first. If you know the *London Times* crosswords, they are the sort that people usually take a week to finish. *Steve and Lenny did them in an afternoon.*

When *New York* magazine was founded in the 1960s, Sondheim introduced English-style cryptics to America in the first issue, along with an entertaining article telling readers how to solve clues. For about a year, he contributed a puzzle every week to the magazine, then for several years, one every three weeks, and finally, when *Company* was going into rehearsal, he stopped. I, a lyricist and director of musicals, had by then become addicted to the verbal games in cryptic clues, and I asked whether I might take over from him. I did, for about ten years, later switching to *Harper's Magazine* where I do a monthly puzzle to this day.

When I started contributing puzzles, I found that I was not alone in my addiction. I was surprised to find that a number of famous show authors did the puzzles regularly. Stephen Schwartz (*Pippin, Wicked*) and Sheldon Harnick (*Fiddler on the Roof, Fiorello!*) used to share notes and grade me on clues.

On a certain level, it makes sense. Lyric-writing is a process in which language is maneuvered technically in order to make meaning conform to the rigors of preordained contours—that is, the melody. It is inherently a word game.

All of this is simply to acknowledge that musicals and game-playing seem to be cut from the same cloth. Trivia games are immensely popular among the companies of musicals, and campy parodies of musicals that show folk love to invent thrive on how many obscure references people can pick up on and laugh at.

Enter Peter Filichia. He has used his many years as a distinguished theater critic to amass a seemly endless quantity of delightful and utterly useless theater information. I have several times tried to play can-you-top-this with Peter—such as what obscure actress was the second replacement for the ingenue in the touring company of some show. I lose every time.

Peter has taken the old impromptu party game of trying to stump people with theater trivia and has raised it to Olympian heights.

Peter would have you believe he was forced by popular demand from the audience of his podcasts to raise the stakes of musical trivia as he has done in this book. Don't you believe it. This is pure and simple naked competitiveness. Which—let's admit it—is not really an impulse to be ashamed of.

I confess that when I attempted to take on the challenge of this book, I got about twenty of the answers without cheating, and even twenty may be a lie. Peter suggests a point system (with fun levels) to make solving the clues into a traditional game, and that is a useful suggestion. But even as a proper game, it strikes me that any reader acquiring this book—you, the idiot reading this, trivia lover that you are—will have to decide how exactly to play it.

I think it is best played in one of four ways.

First, you can play it yourself. Sit alone, read the questions, take as long as you need to figure out the answers, and reward yourself with Cheetos and a glass of Chablis. This is undeniably relaxing. Doing it solitaire also has the advantage of allowing you to cheat. Who is going to tell on you? But it also robs you of the thrill of knowing more than someone else, so unless you are supremely chill and confident about your stature in the world, you may prefer one of the other versions.

Second, you can do it with a friend or your partner. This introduces competitiveness and the prospect of proving your superiority over someone. It also introduces the attraction of any sporting event: winning. If you are someone for whom winning is the point of life, this Bud's for you!

Third, you can make a real party game out of it, with a crowd divided into teams, like charades. This is an obvious choice. People screaming out ideas, jumping up and down, and perhaps, racing the clock is instantaneous fun. The clock is a necessity because without it one team can lose all interest while their opponents go on some endless trivia wild goose chase. One can't argue with this choice, though it does depend on who you have invited to the party. With certain groups (you know who you are!), this kind of game can't lose.

And fourth, a whole room challenge. Unlikely as it might seem, I would suggest that this may actually be the most satisfying choice of all. Charades and other team party games work because all the players share some kind of common knowledge—of book titles, for example. The information in Peter's questions is going to be unknown even to some insiders. The fun, therefore, is getting information from one know-it-all to add to something contributed by another one until the answer gets located. Under these circumstances, the knowledge contributed by one smart-ass after another becomes a collective joy, a group exhilaration. All share! What could be more satisfying than that?

Here is how it would work: turn the whole room into a team, with the moderator guiding and occasionally giving hints: "Yes, *West Side Story*—but who?" "Tony?" "Yes. But what does he sing?" "You're getting warm, in which act?" The arcana in Peter's questions is more rarefied than that of other games. Make a strength of it.

This model has several attractions. It doesn't leave half the room out for long stretches. It does, however, give up the idea of winners— although you can award points to the person who actually yells out the answer. But it also means there aren't losers either, and that can leave a whole room feeling satisfied.

With these instructions in mind, go ahead and buy this book. Or if you have just opened it as a gift from someone you thought was a friend, send out the invitations. When you have your first go around with this book, I guarantee that you will thank Peter Filichia for providing you with a new trivia game that opens entertaining doors that you didn't know existed.

Richard Maltby Jr.

INTRODUCTION

My Fair Lady was previously called *My Lady Liza*.

Feeling Electric was the original title of *next to normal* (which writers Tom Kitt and Brian Yorkey prefer to appear in all lower-case letters).

You knew those facts, right? As Major Strasser says in *Casablanca*, "I expected no less."

And why, you ask, should a film, even one as celebrated as *Casablanca*, be in a book that offers brainteasers about Broadway? Well, you do know, don't you, that *Casablanca* was once a play called *Everybody Comes to Rick's*—one that hadn't been produced prior to its film version?

Even if that choice tidbit somehow escaped your vast depository of knowledge, you still believe that you know quite a bit about Broadway.

For the last dozen years or so, many of you have proved it by answering the questions I've asked at the conclusion of each *Broadway Radio* podcast (www.broadwayradio.com) on which I appear most Sunday mornings. This weekly feature started innocuously enough. During the course of the week, answers would trickle in by email.

But before long, matters became very competitive. Some knew that the podcast, taped at 10 a.m., would go live at 4 p.m., and they were there to send their answers rushing into my inbox within minutes. For some, that wasn't good enough. When host James Marino offered listeners the chance to tune in live, many took that option just so they could be the first to answer. Understand that there was no official prize—just the glory of knowing the answer and getting a mention on the following week's podcast. And yet, many answered.

These are people much like you who are familiar with the smash hits on the level of *The Phantom of the Opera* as well as the smash flops on the low level of *Breakfast at Tiffany's*. (And you know as well as they that both of those musicals played the Majestic Theatre, right?)

You also know songs ranging from "First Midnight" in *Into the Woods* to "The Last Night of the World" from *Miss Saigon*. You know that Freb Ebb used "307 West 4th" as the address where Flora the Red Menace lived because it was actually John Kander's home at the time. And you'll never forget that *Follies* lost the 1971–1972 Best Musical Tony to *Two Gentlemen of Verona*.

These are *facts*. I've got no ax to grind against them, but they simply involve memorization. Granted, I admire that your head holds 525,600 pieces of arcane Broadway information, but in this book, they'll only take you so far.

For we're not just talking *trivia*; we're talking *brainteasers*, which take trivia questions to a higher level. Sorry, Millie Dilmount, who demanded "Gimme, Gimme," but there are few if any gimmes here. Instead, you'll encounter questions that will force you to "Use Your Noggin," to quote the song in the 1966–1967 musical *Walking Happy*.

Such as . . .

He won one Tony each in two different musicals that played the same theater. What he said to end the first act of the first of these musicals—a revival—was the same word that he said in the second act of the second musical—a new work.

In that second instance, though, he said it in the middle of a song.

Who's the actor?

What were the musicals that got him the Tonys?

What word did he say in each?

Some of you have it already. The others who don't know can make a trip to the library or, much more likely, to www.ibdb.com, or—needless to say—the Internet.

At any of these sites you'll discover that only nine men (as of this writing) have won two Tonys as Best Actor in a Musical: Norbert Leo Butz, John Cullum, Richard Kiley, Nathan Lane, Zero Mostel, James Naughton, Robert Preston, George Rose, and Phil Silvers.

However, further research will show you that only Nathan Lane won for two musicals at the same theater: The St. James. There Lane was Pseudolus in the 1996 revival of *A Funny Thing Happened on the Way to the Forum* as well as Max Bialystock in the 2001 hit *The Producers*.

You may remember that at the end of act 1 in *Forum,* Pseudolus says "Intermission!" to get himself out of trouble. But soon you will remember *or find* that in act 2 of *The Producers* during the song "Betrayed"—which is a summary of what has occurred in the musical to that point—Max says "Intermission!" and takes a seat as if the "show" has reached the halfway mark.

Now it's your turn to take a seat—probably, but not necessarily, next to your computer—and see if you can rack up the points. To paraphrase a lyric in *The King and I,* you may be as smart as you think you are. Or, at the very worst, the Internet makes for some Happy Hunting.

And don't worry that even one question will ask you to mention *all* the producers of some current musical. Nobody—not even our most faithful *Broadway Radio* stars—could be expected to know *that* many names.

DEDICATION

Q. What opening number from a late 1970s Tony-nominated musical could describe a certain group of people?

A. The opening number of *The Best Little Whorehouse in Texas* is "20 Fans"—meaning the rotating devices that were planted in the brothel's ceilings to bring cool air into each boudoir.

But for our purposes, "fans" means something different—the fans of *Broadway Radio* who listen intently each Sunday and wait until the end of the show to hear a Brainteaser.

This book is dedicated to twenty of those fans: Steve Bell, Isaac Blevins, Brigadude, Joanna Ebeezee, Mike Ewanus, Juliet Green, Josh Israel, Tony Janicki, Robb Johnston, Cathy Jones, Jay Aubrey Jones, Nikki Juvan, Greg Kristensen, Jack Lechner, Robert LoBiondo, Shawn Logan, Mike Meaney, Deb Poppel, Jeff Vellenga, and Paul Witte.

To all of them—and you—Be happy! Be healthy! Long life!

But before we officially start . . .

SCORING

The book is divided into three sections.

First comes "It's the Hard-Knock Life." For each hard question you answer correctly, give yourself a point.

Next comes "Try Just a Little Bit Harder." Two points here for each correct answer to a *very* hard question.

Finally, there's "I'm a Genius Genius." Yes, as you've inferred, these are three-pointers to *extraordinarily* hard questions.

Get a pencil and a pad and figure it out. Here's the scoring system:

0–100 = Baby
101–200 = Putting It Together
201–300 = Ain't Too Proud
301–400 = Applause
401–500 = The Happy Time
501–600 = Beautiful
601–700 = Fame
701–800 = Hallelujah, Baby!
801–900 = Big Fish
901–1,000 = In the Heights
1,001 plus = I Love You! You're Perfect! *Don't* Change!

IT'S THE HARD-KNOCK LIFE

1Q. What do these musicals have in common?

1) *Applause,* 2) *Come from Away,* 3) *Falsettos,* 4) *Hairspray,* 5) *Pretty Woman,* 6) *Seesaw,* 7) Michael John LaChiusa's *The Wild Party,* 8) *Sweet Smell of Success,* and 9) *Something Rotten!*

2Q. A character in a famous Sondheim musical has a name that is also the title of a musical in which Patti LuPone played the title role. What is it?

3Q. What do these twenty-first-century musicals have in common— something most twenty-first-century musicals don't, but plenty of twentieth-century ones did?

1) *Aladdin,* 2) *Dear Evan Hansen,* 3) *Hadestown,* 4) *Hamilton,* 5) *Kinky Boots,* 6) *Wicked,* 7) *Mean Girls,* 8) *Legally Blonde,* and 9) *Avenue Q.*

4Q. A musical theater song, heard on Broadway both in this century and last, takes place on the 13th, 16th, 21st, and 24th of a certain month.

What's the song?

From what musical does it come?

5Q. Two songs from twenty-first-century musicals have almost identical five-word titles. The first four words of each song are identical; only the last word in each song is different. Those last words are antonyms.

Each song is a duet, and the same performer was involved in both shows' Broadway productions. However, in the first instance, he duetted with a man; in the second, he duetted with a woman. For the first, he won a Best Actor in a Musical Tony; for the second, he didn't even receive a nomination.

Who is he?

What are the musicals?

What are the almost identically titled songs?

6Q. What do these musicals have in common?

1) *Dear World,* 2) *Rachael Lily Rosenbloom and Don't You Ever Forget It,* 3) *Leader of the Pack,* 4) *Rodgers + Hammerstein's Cinderella,* 5) *The 25th Annual Putnam County Spelling Bee,* 6) *Waitress,* and 7) *Diana.*

7Q. A much-anticipated musical of the 1990s didn't turn out to be the hit that everyone had expected. Drop the final two words of the show's five-word official title—*official title,* mind you—and the three remaining first words would aptly describe its fate.

What's the musical's full title?

What would it be if those final two words were cut?

8Q. What do these Tony-winning performers for the original productions of these shows have in common?

1) *Amadeus,* 2) *A Chorus Line,* 3) *Good People,* 4) *Nice Work If You Can Get It,* 5) *Ragtime,* and 6) *South Pacific.*

9Q. *Sports Illustrated* considers chess a sport. As a result, there are not one but two references to sports in the musical *Chess.*

What's the other sport?

10Q. What character in a Tony-winning musical sees two dead bodies on the floor and has no idea whatsoever that they're her father and mother?

11Q. It was the day on which Sierra Boggess, Lisa Kron, and Tony Goldwyn were born. It's also a day that has a different musical theater significance.

What is it?

12Q. The leading character of a Tony and Pulitzer Prize winning musical has the same name as an actor who played the leading male role in a famous revival for a limited engagement. He almost always goes solely by his first name, but for this Broadway appearance, he officially used his last one, too.

What's the name of the character and the musical?

What's the name of the actor and the musical?

13Q. A character in *Beauty and the Beast* says a famous line from Shakespeare that a character in *Hamilton* sings.

What's the phrase?

From what play by Shakespeare does it come?

14Q. Take the title of *Hadestown.* Split it into two separate words. Replace three letters in the first word and get the name of a notorious flop that nevertheless received a Best Choreography nomination (over the work of a choreographer who was already a living legend at the time).

What's the musical?

15Q. What Tony-winner is mentioned in each of these songs?

1) "A Beat Behind" (*The Goodbye Girl*), 2) "Rainbow High" (*Evita*), 3) "I Want It All" (*Baby*), 4) "One Perfect Moment" (*New Faces of 1956*), and 5) "Opposites" (*Skyscraper*).

16Q. A Tony-winning musical from the 1970s has a title song as well as an overture. Usually when a show has both, the overture proudly showcases the title song. This musical didn't.

What's the musical?

17Q. Many a performer has been known to lie about his or her age. A Broadway legend—one whose life story became a jukebox musical at a time when such a species wasn't in vogue—fibbed about his age the *least* of any performer.

Who is he?

By what amount of time did he lie?

18Q. Ambassador, Plymouth, Hudson, Imperial, and Marquis have not only been the names of Broadway theaters, but they've also been the names of makes of automobiles.

One other theater in the twenty-first century was named for a car. What is it?

What's more, name the one and only show that played there.

19Q. When she appeared in her first book musical on Broadway, she played two distinctly different characters. In her second musical a year later, she doubled her past achievement by playing four distinctly different characters.

Who is she?

What are the names of the two musicals?

What are the names of the six characters in search of an answer?

20Q. Two Tony-winning musicals from different seasons opened in the same calendar year and ran concurrently for a long time. Each had a character that had the same occupation. This was a featured character in the one with a longer run, and the lead in the one with a shorter run.

What are the musicals?

What are the characters' names?

What is their occupation?

21Q. What musical played these theaters in this order?: the Phoenix, the Alvin, the Winter Garden, the Cort, the St. James, and the Broadhurst.

22Q. He won a Tony in a twenty-first-century Tony-winning musical, but in it, he sang a little bit of a song that was the title tune of a 1930s musical film.

What's the song?

From what film does it come?

Who sang it this century?

In what musical did he sing it?

23Q. Many musicals tell the story of a family. Sometimes actors who play fathers win Tonys—such as Michael Cerveris in *Fun Home.*

Sometimes actresses who portray mothers emerge victorious–such as Alice Ripley in *next to normal.*

Sometimes actors and actresses who play children win—such as John Gallagher Jr. in *Spring Awakening* and Anika Noni Rose in *Caroline, Or Change.*

But what musical saw performers who played members of *an entire family* receive Tony awards?

While you're at it, name the family members and who played them.

24Q. This real-life personality was prominently mentioned in a 1990s Tony-nominated Best Musical. One of her husbands was mentioned in a song in *South Pacific*; a later one was mentioned in *Little Me.*

Who is she?

Who were the husbands?

In what songs were they mentioned?

25Q. A minor movie personality was mentioned in what became Broadway's longest-running musical. Later, he was also mentioned in the show that eclipsed that musical as the longest-running one.

Who is he?

What are the musicals?

In what songs is he mentioned?

26Q. A song from a very famous musical mentions people who hailed from Arkansas, Kansas, Maine, Michigan, New York, Texas, and Wisconsin.

What is the name of the song?

From what musical does it come?

27Q. One musical is set in a locale that's a mashup of the fifteenth and twentieth states to be admitted into the union.

What's the locale?

What musical takes place there?

28Q. The title of this Tony-nominated play is the name of one of the 366 days of the year in which it opened on Broadway. You might think that it would debut on the actual date of the title, but instead it opened precisely four months after the date cited.

What is it?

When did it open?

(And, yes, that the year had 366 days in it can serve as a hint.)

29Q. What do Alvin, Bernie, Charlie, Ezekiel, and Wilmer have in common?

30Q. Whose very famous and distinctive voice is the first to be heard on the original cast album of *Funny Girl*?

31Q. What smash hit musical mentions Alice Cooper, Betty Crocker, Karen Horney, Jascha Heifetz, Conrad Hilton, Carlo Ponti, Gloria Steinem, Levi Strauss, and Joanne Woodward?

32Q. A twentieth-century musical that starred sisters had a score written by brothers.
   Who were these women?
   Who were these men?
   What was the musical?

33Q. It was a Tony-winning musical that had an overture that was unique in that its first song included the name of its leading male character. The second and third songs had not one but *two* names given to the show's leading female character.
   What were the names of the songs?
   From what overture do they come?

34Q. He wrote the novels that inspired two musicals. In each, the novelist himself was an actual character.
   Who is he?

35Q. There's a song in which the musical's sole female performer mentions three famous musical theater characters: a young Puerto Rican woman, a Jewish father, and an African American who's a native of South Carolina.
   What's the song?
   From what musical does it come?
   What's the name of the character who sings it?
   Who are the three characters mentioned?

36Q. A certain 1960s Tony-nominated Best Musical—one that wound up winning only one Tony in a different category—had a logo that actually pictured the name of the Tony-winning play on which it was based.
   What is it?

37Q. What do these songs have in common?

1) "Miss Marmelstein" (*I Can Get It for You Wholesale*), 2) "When You're Good to Mama" (*Chicago*), 3) "Moving Too Fast" (*The Last 5 Years*), 4) "Oklahoma?" (*Dirty Rotten Scoundrels*), 5) "What You Want" (*Legally Blonde*), 6) "Everything Else" (*next to normal*), and 7) "My Shot" (*Hamilton*).

38Q. As of this writing, what do the theaters named the Booth, Broadhurst, Circle in the Square, Ethel Barrymore, Imperial, Long-acre, Majestic, Marquis, Minskoff, Music Box, New Amsterdam, Palace, Shubert, and Vivian Beaumont have in common?

39Q. What Harold Prince production that centered on a famous fictional character was the first musical to feature a *Playbill* with a color cover?

40Q. What do these musicals have in common?

1) *Coco,* 2) *Two's Company,* 3) *Tovarich,* 4) *Call Me Madam,* 5) *The Girl Who Came to Supper,* 6) *Look to the Lilies,* 7) *Flower Drum Song,* 8) *Minnie's Boys,* 9) *Maggie Flynn,* 10) *The Grand Tour,* and 11) *Triumph of Love.*

41Q. This performer appeared—but not for long—in a show that later won a Best Musical Tony.

More than a dozen years later, in yet another Best Musical Tony-winner, this same performer was mentioned by name in a song. The reason has to do with something that happened to her in that first show.

Who's the performer?

What are the two musicals?

What's the song that mentions her name?

Why was she mentioned?

42Q. This performer's full name is actually mentioned in a song in *Nunsense*. Add an *o* to the middle of her first name, and you'll get the first name of a character in a Tony-winning musical.

(Hint: The septuagenarian who originally played her received a Best Featured Actress in a Musical Tony nomination, but lost to someone else in the cast.)

Who are these two performers?

43Q. A novel from the 1930s was made into a film in the 1950s—but there the sex of the protagonist was changed from a man to a woman. When the musical version of the novel opened in the 1960s, the protagonist was a man again—but a woman wound up stealing the show.

What's the name of the property that never changed?

Who's the woman who stole the musical?

44Q. We're talking about two consecutive Sondheim musicals. What would a character in act 2 of the first one say after hearing the first two words sung in act 1 of the second one?

45Q. A musical that closed on the road in the 1950s had a three-word title. When it was resuscitated in the 1980s to substantial success, it took only the final word of that title and added another word for its new title.

What were the musicals?

46Q. She won a Tony in a musical where she appeared in just one scene and appeared in only one song (and its encore). The song was obviously of great importance to her, for she ensured that when she died its name would be carved on her headstone.

Who is she?

What's the song?

In what musical did she sing it?

47Q. Why are these musicals listed in this order?

1) *The Phantom of the Opera,* 2) *Crazy for You,* 3) *Aladdin,* 4) *A Strange Loop,* 5) *Carrie,* 6) *Chicago,* 7) *Miss Liberty,* 8) *Hairspray,* 9) *Fiddler on the Roof,* 10) *110 in the Shade,* 11) *Anything Goes,* and 12) *Dear Evan Hansen.*

48Q. What do these songs have in common?

1) "Why Can't a Woman Be More Like a Man?" (*My Fair Lady*), 2) "The VD Polka" (*Over Here!*), 3) "I Would Trust Her" (*The Pajama Game*), 4) "Nothing's Gonna Harm You" (*Sweeney Todd*), 5) "Things Could Be Better" (*The Full Monty*), and 6) "What Do I Do Now?" (*Mame*).

49Q. When a world-famous musical began its tryout, it had a song that began act 2—but by the final leg of the two-city tryout, the song was now closing act 2.

(Hint: The name of the song is also the name of the place where the musical is set.)

What's the show?

What's the song?

50Q. You're riding in the passenger seat of a car and you notice a strange sound coming from the front of it. The driver says to you, "I can't figure out what that sound is."

You respond by giving a line that was heard in Wichita's one and only burlesque theater.

What's the line?

51Q. What do these songs have in common?

1) "You're the Top" (*Anything Goes*), 2) "Do It the Hard Way" (*Pal Joey*), 3) "It's a Perfect Relationship" (*Bells Are Ringing*), 4) "The American Dream" (*Miss Saigon*), and 5) "Gentleman Jimmy" (*Fiorello!*).

52Q. A song in a Tony-winning score from the 1960s—but one that failed to win Best Musical—contains two words in a row that many decades later would become the name of a popular Ben and Jerry's Ice Cream flavor.

What are the words?

In what song do they appear?

53Q. You are going to change the first letter of the name of a musical and replace it with one that immediately follows it in the alphabet. For example, if the musical were *Kean—K-e-a-n*—it would become *Lean—L-e-a-n*, because *L* follows *K* in the alphabet.

So give the name of a musical that played Broadway in the twentieth century and encores in the twenty-first. Change one letter in the first word of the title to the next letter alphabetically. Then you'll have a title that would be apt for a musical version of *The Catcher in the Rye.*

What is it?

54Q. Two producers, while readying their new musical, loved the score that their composer-lyricist had written. But they didn't like the book, and replaced the writer; the new librettist rescued the property and turned it into a Best Musical Tony-winning classic.

A bit more than a decade later, the same two producers and the same songwriter found themselves in the same position again and called on the same show doctor to save them. Once again, he rewrote the script, and once again a Tony-winning Best Musical was the result.

Who were the producers?

Who was the songwriter?

Who was the new librettist?

What musicals did he rescue?

55Q. This beloved three-time Tony-nominated musical performer (who could have easily emerged victorious on one occasion had she played her cards differently) married a man whose last name was the same as the first word of the town in which she was born. The marriage didn't last, but the town has.

Who is the performer?

Who was her husband?

56Q. 1) "Getting to Know You" (*The King and I*), 2) "I've Grown Accustomed to Her Face" (*My Fair Lady*), 3) "Standing on the Corner" (*The Most Happy Fella*), 4) "A Lot of Livin' to Do" (*Bye Bye Birdie*), 5) "I'll Never Fall in Love Again" (*Promises, Promises*), and 6) "Send in the Clowns (*A Little Night Music*) were big bona fide pop hits from successful twentieth-century musicals.

And yet, each of these songs missed out on something.

What?

57Q. This composer saw one of his musicals become the longest-running one in Broadway history. This lyricist saw one of his musicals do the same. They eventually collaborated on the score of a 1970s musical.

If pig Latin were applied to its name, you'd get a word that is often heard in hospitals and medical offices.

Who were the writers?

What were their record-breaking musicals?

What's the name of their musical in both English and pig Latin?

58Q. What do these songs have in common?

1) "Colored Lights" (*The Rink*), 2) "One Normal Night" (*The Addams Family*), 3) "What Was a Woman to Do?" (*Dirty Rotten Scoundrels*), 4) "Dance: Ten, Looks: Three" (*A Chorus Line*), and especially 5) "Opening" (*New Faces of 1952*).

59Q. Hamilton is the title character of *Hamilton*. Tina is the title character of *Tina*. But there's one esteemed biomusical in which the subject's name is actually oh-so-slightly different from the name that's seen in the title.

What musical is it?

What's the explanation?

60Q. What do the Tony-winning hits *Cabaret, Fiddler on the Roof, Hello, Dolly!, The King and I,* and *Les Misérables* all have in common?

61Q. This performer's final Broadway appearance was as a replacement in a now-famous musical that has a one-word title.

The title is the first word that began the title of a famous Broadway musical whose film version three decades earlier saw her as the star—after the first choice for the film was fired.

Who is the performer?

Whom did she replace?

What are the musicals?

62Q. A big hit musical that closed as one of twenty longest-running musicals in Broadway history was nominated for seven Tonys, but won only two. One was for Best Lighting.

But if the show hadn't won the other award, why would that loss have been extremely embarrassing?

63Q. His first name is the name of a state capital. So is his last name.

On Broadway he's played an animal as well as the member of a royal family in one musical, a guitar-playing roustabout in another, roller-skated in yet another, and played a porno star in a play.

Who is he?

64Q. One of Broadway's most famous and much revived musicals ends its first act with a song that makes a baseball reference.

The musical almost ends its second act with another song that contains yet another baseball reference.

What's the musical?

What are the songs?

What are the baseball references?

65Q. She didn't appear in the show until the first 45 minutes had passed, and yet she won a Tony as leading actress in a musical.

He had all of one song and yet he won a Tony as leading actor in a musical.

Who are they?

What was the musical?

66Q. He played the same president of the United States in two different musicals. In the first, the character wasn't yet a president; in the second, he indeed was a sitting one.

Who is he?

What was the first musical?

What was the second?

67Q. What long-running, Best Play Tony-nominee—as well as its musical version, which won a Best Musical Tony—has a title that has absolutely *nothing* to do with its plot, characters, or dialogue?

68Q. What do these shows have in common?

1) *Hadestown,* 2) the 1996 revival of *A Funny Thing Happened on the Way to the Forum,* 3) *Pippin,* and 4) *Whose Life Is It Anyway?*

69Q. Two songs have identical titles. They were introduced in musicals that opened a bit more than a decade apart.

The earlier song was sung by a now-legendary performer who did all but the final week of the run.

The later performer did this eleven o'clock number only in Boston, and for that matter, he didn't do the song that replaced it for very long, either.

What's the name of both songs?

From what musicals do they come?

Who were the performers?

Explain why the later performer didn't do the replacement song for very long.

70Q. A Tony-winning musical that she choreographed in the 1950s started its action on the same national holiday as the Tony-winning musical that she choreographed in the 1960s.

Who is she?

What are the musicals?

What date does each musical cover?

71Q. What do these musicals have in common?

1) *Tuck Everlasting,* 2) *The 25th Annual Putnam County Spelling Bee,* 3) *Hamilton,* 4) *Rent,* 5) the 2009 revival of *A Little Night Music,* and 6) the 1964 film version of *My Fair Lady.*

72Q. Richard Kiley, when discussing his New York appearances in *Man of La Mancha,* could define his experience with the musical by using a line from a song in *Company* that a famous star originated.

What is it?

73Q. What do these characters have in common?

1) Coalhouse Walker Jr. (*Ragtime*), 2) Jean Valjean (*Les Misérables*), 3) Frederick Frankenstein (*Young Frankenstein*), 4) Charity Hope Valentine (*Sweet Charity*), 5) Charlie Price (*Kinky Boots*), and 6) Billy Bigelow (*Carousel*).

74Q. What company that has paid to have its name on a theater is also mentioned in a long-running twenty-first-century Tony-nominated musical?

75Q. What do these musicals have in common?

1) The first Broadway revival of *Grease,* 2) the first Broadway revival of *Wonderful Town,* 3) the original production of *Kiss of the Spider Woman,* and 4) the original production of *Hello, Dolly!*

76Q. There's a very famous character from a nineteenth-century Italian novel that became best known through a Walt Disney animated film.

The character's famous song in that movie could also actually be sung by someone who owns an original Broadway (or London) cast album that boasts a 1960s Tony-winning score.

Who's the character?

What's his famous song?

How does it apply to the Tony-winning score?

77Q. For a few months in 1999, two musicals had a song that named a comic strip character.

To be fair and accurate, the musical that ran far, far longer—a jukebox musical—didn't actually cite the comic strip character; it was just referring to someone who had the same name.

What's the name of the character and the song?

What are the two musicals?

78Q. What do these musicals have in common?

1) *Annie,* 2) *Fiddler on the Roof,* 3) *I Had a Ball,* 4) *On the Town,* and 5) *Pal Joey.*

79Q. His real first name was Adolph, but he changed it by the time of his second Broadway appearance in 1925.

His new name was also the name of a character in a twenty-first-century musical.

What was Adolph's more famous name?

What was the twenty-first-century musical that had a character with the same name?

80Q. Why are these performers listed in this order?

1) Graham Phillips, 2) Susan Watson, 3) Ann-Margret, 4) Lauri Peters, 5) Lea Salonga, and 6) Barry Bostwick.

81Q. This librettist-lyricist didn't officially give names to his romantically linked leading characters, although if you listened long and hard enough at this off-Broadway musical, you would have heard their actual names.

Who's the writer?

What's the musical?

What are the official names of the main characters?

82Q. What song in a musical celebrates two baseball Hall of Famers—one who played mostly for the Detroit Tigers and the other who pitched for the Dodgers, both when they were in Brooklyn as well as in Los Angeles?

83Q. An Oscar-winning film of the 1930s was made into a Tony-nominated musical of the 1980s.

And yet, one of the movie's most remembered lines—one that often shows up on lists of Hollywood's most famous film quotations—was used neither in dialogue nor in a lyric in the musical.

What's the line?

What's the film?

What's the musical?

84Q. What do these songs have in common?

1) "Piragua" (*In the Heights*), 2) "When It Dries" (*Two by Two*), 3) "Song of the Sand" (*La Cage aux Folles*), 4) "Popular" (*Wicked*), 5) "Do Something" (*Honeymoon in Vegas*), 6) "A Musical" (*Something Rotten!*), 7) "Working It Out" (*They're Playing Our Song*), and 8) "You'll Be Back" (*Hamilton*).

85Q. In act 1, scene 9, we're specifically told that this character has grown twenty-three inches since act 1, scene 5.

Who's the character?

What's the musical?

86Q. The vast majority of book musicals haven't had a female lyricist. And yet, a Broadway musical of a famous play sported two female lyricists, one of whom succeeded the other.

　　Who are they?

　　What is the musical?

87Q. A song called "Can't Lovin' Be Fun?" is mentioned in the title song of a 1970s Tony-nominated musical.

　　Tell how and why.

88Q. What John Kander song has the same name as a musical that was seen in lower Manhattan in 2022?

89Q. If writers had followed the lead of a Tony-winning play, we'd have musicals with such names as 1) *Joshua on Joshua,* 2) *The Penn Adair Follies,* 3) *Wilson's Broadway,* and 4) *Sunday in the Park with Pierre.*

　　Explain.

90Q. This performer won a Tony in the 1950s for appearing in a musical in which he played a character whose name we never really know.

　　Who's the performer?

　　What's the role?

　　What's the musical?

91Q. If you said "January 8, 1911" to the title character of a 1950s Tony-nominated musical, you wouldn't quite answer the question she had asked, but you'd have given her a solid hint on what she wanted to know.

　　Why?

92Q. This performer was a member of the original cast of three Broadway musicals that eventually ran for over five thousand performances. He also appeared in the film version of a different Broadway musical that also ran over five thousand performances.

Who's the performer?

What are the three Broadway musicals?

What is the film version?

93Q. Considering the three famous plays he wrote, could we infer that he wrote one that he set in New Mexico but never let be produced?

All right, this is a joke, but see if you can find the explanation.

94Q. Why are these songs in this order?

1) "Ilona" (*She Loves Me*), 2) "Day One" (*Groundhog Day*), 3) "Windy City" (*Windy City*), 4) "Conga!" (*Wonderful Town*), 5) "Frankie's Testimony" (*Parade*), 6) "A Cockeyed Optimist" (*South Pacific*), 7) "All American" (*Stop the World—I Want to Get Off*), 8) "Everything I Know" (*In the Heights*), 9) "I'm Just Taking My Time" (*Subways Are for Sleeping*), 10) "It's Your Wedding Day" (*The Wedding Singer*), 11) "To Break in a Glove" (*Dear Evan Hansen*), and 12) "Good Friends" (*Applause*).

95Q. Jason in *Falsettos* and the elder Mr. Price in *Kinky Boots* would disagree on a certain issue.

What is it?

96Q. Many male luminaries who won Tonys made their mark in famous roles returned to Broadway in revivals: Richard Kiley in *Man of La Mancha,* John Cullum in *Shenandoah,* Zero Mostel in *Fiddler on the Roof.*

But there are two female luminaries who did *not* win a Tony for playing characters whom they'd later play again on Broadway in a different context, fully acknowledging that the characters had aged.

Who are they?

What are their characters?

What are the first musicals and the subsequent ones?

97Q. What do these Best Musical Tony-winners have in common?

1) *Wonderful Town,* 2) *Applause,* 3) *Ain't Misbehavin',* 4) *42nd Street,* 5) *The Will Rogers Follies,* 6) *Crazy for You,* 7) *Passion,* 8) *Fosse,* and 9) *Contact.*

98Q. Sondheim wrote a lyric for a song in *Gypsy* that was eventually dropped. Given its title—and considering a lyric in a song that Sondheim would write for *Into the Woods*—we could thus judge Rose as a good person.

Explain.

99Q. She's seen not one, not two, but three performers win Oscars for roles that she originated on stage.

Who is she?

What were the musicals?

Who won the Oscars instead of her?

100Q. What do these characters found in musicals have in common?

1) Lily Garland (*On the Twentieth Century*), 2) Joe Hardy (*Damn Yankees*), 3) Eve Harrington (*Applause*), 4) Harold Hill (*The Music Man*), 5) Paul San Marco (*A Chorus Line*), and 6) Signor Pirelli and 7) Sweeney Todd (both in *Sweeney Todd*).

101Q. When a musical movie becomes a Broadway musical, we expect that it will use the film's most famous songs in its overture to remind the audience of the score's riches.

But what overture that's more than three minutes long has no songs from its famous film?

102Q. What do these lesser-known (and less successful) Tennessee Williams plays have in common?

1) *Orpheus Descending,* 2) *The Seven Descents of Myrtle,* 3) *27 Wagons Full of Cotton,* and 4) *The Milk Train Doesn't Stop Here Anymore.*

103Q. An actress who had originated two roles on Broadway saw the same actress replace her in both of those roles in the two film versions.

Who's the stage actress?

Who succeeded her?

What were the films?

104Q. This performer had a musical written about her. The composer of that show had five years earlier written a musical—also about a performer—in which the subject of the later musical was mentioned in a lyric.

Who's the subject of the musical?

What's its name?

How is she mentioned in a lyric in the earlier musical?

105Q. Grant, Alvarez, and DeLeon. Why are these names in this order and why are they lumped together?

106Q. When *She Loves Me* opened on Broadway in 1963, its opening song "Good Morning, Good Day" included the lyric "Wouldn't it be something if we all took off from work leaving Mr. Maraczek without a single clerk?"

But a year later, in preparation for a London opening, Sheldon Harnick changed the lyric to "Wonder what would happen if we did just run away? We could leave a note that said we won't be in today."

Why?

107Q. What character in a musical made a financial estimate for 1959, followed by another character who did the same for both 1964 and 1974?

108Q. What do these shows have in common?

1) *Legally Blonde,* 2) *Love Letters,* 3) *On Your Toes,* 4) *Ragtime,* 5) *Rent,* and 6) *Starlight Express*?

109Q. He's a character who establishes himself by name in the first words he delivers in this musical.

  Who is he?

  What's the musical?

110Q. A theater that was one of the first to open in what we now call the theater district stopped housing plays during the Great Depression and switched to films.

  Many decades later, its insides were gutted to make way for a new theater. Since its reopening, it endured many name changes. As of this writing, the theater again has the name that it originally had.

  What is it?

  What were the previous names?

111Q. What do these musicals have in common?

  1) *Allegro,* 2) *Les Misérables,* 3) *Miss Saigon,* and 4) *Rent.*

112Q. Many songs rhyme "wife" with "life," which is understandable, for a wife is supposed to stay around for life.

  But there's one long song from a Tony-winning classic that uses "life" (thirteen times), "knife," and "strife," but never "wife"—which is surprising because the point of the song is that strife occurs between men and women before and after marriage.

  What's the song?

  What's the musical?

113Q. What do these Tony-winning musicals have in common?

  1) *The Music Man,* 2) *Les Misérables,* 3) *Avenue Q,* and 4) *Hamilton.*

114Q. When an Oscar-winning movie was turned into a Tony-winning musical, one of the film's character names had to be changed.

  What's the film and the musical?

  What was the character's original name?

  To what was it changed and why?

115Q. Although Joe Boyd in *Damn Yankees* is a rabid Washington Senators fan, he doesn't live in the nation's capital.

The nearby town in which he and his wife do live, however, has the same name as a performer who was in a 1973 off-Broadway revue that took its name from a national humor magazine.

What's the town that has the same name as the performer?

What was the off-Broadway musical called?

116Q. Leo Bloom in *The Producers* sings about a certain place he'd like to visit on a regular basis. This establishment once had an affinity with a similar place where Helene in *Sweet Charity* said that she'd like to work.

What are the names of both establishments?

117Q. What do these songs have in common?

1) "All I Need Is the Girl" (*Gypsy*), 2) "I Cannot Hear the City" (*Sweet Smell of Success*), and 3) "Ironic" (*Jagged Little Pill*).

118Q. This is going to be a trick question. When *Seesaw* began its out-of-town tryout in Detroit, it had two stars in the cast. When it left Detroit, both were gone.

Explain.

119Q. Throughout the 1970s and 1980s, many Broadway theaters had the same words on their marquees.

How could this be possible?

120Q. The first name of this entertainer served as the title of this 1960s biomusical that closed so quickly that it was denied an original cast album. (Not that any record company had signed to do it.)

However, a dozen years later, this entertainer's first and last names were mentioned in a song in a musical that ran more than 110 times longer. If you think that's something, its revival has run more than 1,300 times longer.

What was the biomusical?

On whom was it based?

What's the name of the song and the musical that mentioned her?

121Q. What do these musicals have in common?

1) *Café Crown,* 2) *The Goodbye Girl,* 3) *Rags,* and 4) *Hallelujah, Baby!*

122Q. In its Boston tryout, this comedy had a different title from the one that it acquired before it became a smash hit on Broadway and a Pulitzer Prize winner.

At first, it was named for what this character was; in the end, it was named for the character.

What was the original title?

What was the eventual one?

123Q. Some songs in musicals have grammatically incorrect titles: "Ain't Got No" (*Hair*), "Her Is" (*The Pajama Game*), and "I'll Learn Ya" (*Let It Ride!*).

One song from a world-famous musical—a song that wasn't included in its film version—made a grammatical error by omitting just a single letter.

What's the song?

From what musical does it come?

124Q. It's a comedy that requires fourteen actors, but for its 1986 revival, twenty-six performers took curtain calls.

Why?

What's the comedy?

125Q. What do these characters have in common?

1) Gloria Upson (*Mame*), 2) David Jordan (*No Strings*), 3) Lizzie Borden (*New Faces of 1952*), 4) Josiah Bartlett (*1776*), 5) Lola (*Damn Yankees*), and 6) Hazel Flagg in her own musical.

126Q. We see Sweeney Todd kill in the double figures. Perhaps he even murdered in the triple figures; we'll never know.

But we are told (if not shown) that a very famous character in one classic play and many musical adaptations (none of them successful) did kill in the triple figures.

Who?

127Q. In one of Broadway's longest-running shows, two twentieth-century presidents, one of whom succeeded the other, may come to mind when you're listening to its eleven o'clock number.

The first president's first name is mentioned; the second one's famous nickname follows.

Who are they?

What's the song?

From what musical does it come?

128Q. He wrote the music for shows that had scenes set in such states as California, Kansas, Illinois, Maryland, New Mexico, Nebraska, New Jersey, New York (several times), Ohio, Vermont, and Washington.

With all those, you might not expect that he'd compose all the music for a Broadway musical that was set completely in England. On second thought, though, that setting was actually most apt.

Who is he?

Why was a show set in England not necessarily a stretch?

129Q. What song by one of Broadway's most famous songwriting teams was written in the 1930s, sung by Elvis Presley in the 1950s, became a number one hit for three weeks in the 1960s, and was briefly heard in the film of *Grease* in the 1970s?

130Q. Why are these shows in this order? 1) *Breakfast at Tiffany's,* 2) *Kelly,* 3) *Next Time I'll Sing to You,* 4) *Oh, Brother!,* 5) *Rags,* 6) *Carrie,*

7) *Carnival in Flanders,* 8) *Buttrio Square,* 9) *The Conquering Hero,* 10) *Anyone Can Whistle,* and 11) *Tommy Tune Tonite!*

131Q. A certain song from a Pulitzer Prize–winning musical would be apt to play during the first week of February—especially if you lived in the second state that was admitted to the union.
Explain.

132Q. Aside from the fact that both *The Cradle Will Rock* and *Lolita, My Love* had trouble opening, what else did they have in common?

133Q. During the 1960s, a film of a 1950s Broadway musical starred three performers. The first-billed would later do the lead in a film version of a drama by a playwright who's had a theater named after him.
The second-billed would later direct a film version of a smash Broadway musical. The third would much later become the subject of a musical that played London, but, at least as of this writing, has never been on Broadway.
What's the film?
Who were the three stars?
Name the properties described above.

134Q. Aside from locales where theatrical productions have played, what do Broadway, Cape Cod, Grand Street, Greenwich Village, London, and Provincetown all have in common?
(Hint: A Sondheim musical is part of the answer.)

135Q. Soon after he won a Tony for appearing in a Tony-winning musical, he went on to star in a very successful television series that bore his name.
Ten years after he'd picked up his award, a soon-to-be legendary musical opened in which a married couple had the same first names as the television show's male supporting character and female supporting character, too.

For that matter, the female supporting character's last name in the television show was the maiden name of the wife of the *other* couple in the show.

What's the Tony-winning musical?

Who's the Tony-winner?

What's the name of the television show?

What are the names of all these characters?

In what musical did they appear?

136Q. What do these songs have in common?

1) "Johnny One-Note" (*Babes in Arms*), 2) "Live and Let Live" (*Can-Can*), 3) "Thinking" (*Do I Hear a Waltz?*), and 4) "Everything Else" (*next to normal*).

137Q. What 1960s Tony-nominated Best Musical that has been revived both in the twentieth and twenty-first century has an important prop that's also the name of a Broadway theater?

138Q. The opening number of a Sondheim Best Musical Tony-winner (and Best Musical Revival Tony-winner) actually happens to mention the title of a previous Sondheim musical.

What's the name of the song?

What's the name of the musical that is mentioned in another context?

139Q. In a musical that won her a Best Actress in a Musical Tony, she played a character whose first name was spelled the same as hers—but it was pronounced differently.

What was the musical?

What are the identically spelled names?

What was the atypical pronunciation?

140Q. What do these musicals have in common?

1) *Allegro*, 2) *Carousel*, 3) *Dreamgirls*, 4) *Grey Gardens*, 5) *Mr. Saturday Night*, 6) *Ragtime*, and 7) *The Will Rogers Follies*.

141Q. A simple spoken line in the first scene of a famous multi-Tony-winning 1960s musical was the impetus for the show's composer-lyricist to write a new song for the film version using that line as his title. It replaced his leading lady's original opening song.

(Hint: The film song was sung by someone who'd recently won an Oscar; the stage song had been sung by someone who'd recently been an Oscar-nominee.)

What's the song?

What's the film?

What song did it replace?

Who were the stars in question?

142Q. A Best Musical Tony-winner—and another that received seven Tony nominations—were both very successful commercially. The former ran for years on and off Broadway; the latter was broadcast on MTV during its year-plus run.

Despite their popularity, these musicals weren't nearly as successful (and not nearly as awarded) as a late twentieth-century film that each musical mentions in a song.

What's the film?

What are the musicals?

What are the names of the songs?

143Q. What do these musicals—later made into films—have in common?

1) *A Little Night Music,* 2) *Mame,* 3) *The Music Man,* 4) *1776,* 5) *Sweet Charity,* and 6) *Too Many Girls.*

144Q. What do these performers have in common?

1) Tammy Grimes, 2) James Monroe Iglehart, 3) Alan Paul, 4) Carol Sawyer, and 5) David Wayne.

145Q. What do these musicals have in common?

1) *Juno,* 2) *Whoop-Up,* 3) *Greenwillow,* 4) *The Pajama Game,* and 5) *How to Succeed in Business Without Really Trying.*

146Q. In *The Music Man*, the first time—the *very* first time—that the four enemies who'll become a barbershop quartet do any singing, they bring to mind a song that a Tony-winner from *The Music Man*'s original 1957 production would sing nearly six years later in a Tony-nominated musical.

What do the four men *first* sing?

What's the song that the Tony-winner sang in the subsequent musical?

From what musical did that song come?

Who is that performer who had a history with *The Music Man*?

147Q. Why are these musicals in this order?

1) The 2017 revival *of Hello, Dolly!* 2) *Ragtime,* 3) *Ghost,* and 4) *Caroline, or Change.*

148Q. We don't associate this performer with Broadway, although he did win a Tony Award in the 1950s. Within two years, he would have the first long-playing record to sell over one million copies, albeit with songs that sounded quite different from the Broadway songs of that era.

Who is he?

In what show did he perform?

149Q. What songs from these musicals offer what we'll euphemistically call alternative facts?

1) *Fiddler on the Roof,* 2) *110 in the Shade,* 3) *You're a Good Man, Charlie Brown,* and 4) *How Now, Dow Jones.*

150Q. A 1980s Broadway musical had a song that, when translated into English, was rebutted by a 1990s British musical produced by Cameron Mackintosh and based on a world-famous novel that Orson Welles had already fashioned into a Broadway play.

What's the Broadway musical?

What's the British musical?

What's the song from the Broadway musical that's corrected by the British one?

151Q. In "Better," the act 2 opener of *A Class Act,* Edward Kleban, the show's subject, exclaims "Barbra Streisand is recording one of my songs!"

What's ironic about the statement?

152Q. What do *Candide, Me and Juliet,* and an early 1960s short-running musical have in common?

153Q. One of Broadway's greatest writers (who did very well as a director, too) once made an observation about a certain type of play or musical.

If he were alive today, he'd be forced to change the last two words of his famous seven-word observation, thanks to a change in the scheduling of shows.

What is the quotation?
What would it be now?
Who said it?

154Q. Two characters in *The King and I* are addressed as "Sir."
Who are they?

155Q. What do the musicals *Canterbury Tales, Celebration,* and *Zorba,* all recorded by Capitol Records, all from the 1968–1969 season, have in common?

156Q. "Arabian Nights" in *Aladdin,* "Hello!" in *The Book of Mormon,* "No One Mourns the Wicked" in *Wicked* are all opening numbers in which you hear those titles of the songs as lyrics in the song.

However, one composer-lyricist titled the opening numbers of his first two hit musicals—his *only* two hit musicals—with words that do not show up in the songs.

What are the musicals?

What are the songs?

Who wrote them?

157Q. When an established musical theater classic was revived this century, the songwriting team added a new song to its score. The song also happens to have the same name of a film biography of two nineteenth-century musical theater greats.

What are the names of both teams?

What's the musical into which the new song was inserted?

On whom does the film biography center?

158Q. The friendship between these two superstars started in the 1960s and spurred them to appear together in three TV specials— one in that decade and one in each of the ensuing ones.

In the 1990s, one opened in an off-Broadway musical; then, when the show moved to Broadway six years later, the other performer assumed the role.

Who are they?

What was the musical?

159Q. What do these alphabetically arranged Tony-winning song- writers have in common?

1) Jerry Bock, 2) Marvin Hamlisch, 3) Sheldon Harnick, 4) Jerry Herman, 5) Edward Kleban, and 6) Maury Yeston.

160Q. A famous musical from the 1940s had a title song that ended with a certain punctuation mark. A less-celebrated but long-running musical from the early twenty-first century had a *song* with the same name, but it ended with different punctuation mark.

What's the name of the song?

What are the two musicals?

What are the different punctuation marks?

161Q. This composer-lyricist put in the opening number of his musical (one that would win him a Best Score Tony) three words in six notes from a song he'd written before.

Who is he?

What's the musical?

What's the song within the song?

162Q. To say the least, Rodgers and Hammerstein weren't known for unadulterated rock 'n' roll. And yet, they apparently wrote such a song in one of their musicals that even used the words "rock" and "roll."

What's the song?

From what musical does it come?

163Q. In the 1970s, a musical trying out in New England had a six-word title that was named for a song in the show.

By the show's next tryout stop, the musical's title had been shortened; the last five words of its original title had been dropped. The song, however, remained in the score and kept all five words through its multiyear Tony-nominated run.

What was the musical's eventual title?

What was the name of the song that had been the title?

164Q. Why wouldn't Henrik of *A Little Night Music* like these songs? For the same reason, why wouldn't he like a certain Tony-winning musical?

1) "Bloody Mary" (*South Pacific*), 2) "I Am the One" (*next to normal*), 3) "I've Got Your Number" (*Little Me*), 4) "Old Friends" (*Merrily We Roll Along*), 5) "Do It Alone" (*Parade*), and 6) "I've Grown Accustomed to Her Face" (*My Fair Lady*).

165Q. What do these musicals have in common?

1) *Here's Love*, 2) *The Light in the Piazza*, 3) *Barnum*, and 4) *Rugantino*?

166Q. In a fanciful and whimsical manner of speaking, what Tony-nominated musical of the 1960s could be said to have been a jukebox musical?

PART TWO

QUESTIONS

TRY JUST A LITTLE BIT HARDER

167Q. How do these songs, when taken together, *in a way* encompass the entire world?

1) "Piddle, Twiddle and Resolve" (*1776*), 2) "Donna" (*Hair*), 3) "Leadville Johnny Brown's Soliloquy" (*The Unsinkable Molly Brown)*, 4) "As We Stumble Along" (*The Drowsy Chaperone)*, 5) "I Like America" (*Ace of Clubs*), 6) "Two by Two" (*The Book of Mormon*), and 7) "Molasses to Rum" (*1776*).

168Q. Three men from the original cast of a Kander and Ebb musical had a big second act number. One performer had already won a Tony. One would soon win a Tony for this very show. One had to wait quite a few years for a Tony.

Who are the three performers?

For what musicals did they win?

What's the song?

From what musical does it come?

169Q. The following all suggest that something Stephen Sondheim once alleged in a song is true.

1) "What Do the Simple Folk Do?" (*Camelot*), 2) "Nowadays" (*Chicago*), 3) "A Secretary Is Not a Toy" (*How to Succeed in Business Without Really Trying*), 4) "Pretty Women" (*Sweeney Todd*), and 5) "The Merry Little Minuet"—sometimes simply known as "The Merry Minuet" (*John Murray Anderson's Almanac*).

What is it?

170Q. This Tony-nominated musical with one of the most famous and beloved logos in all of Broadway history opened precisely on the thirtieth birthday of the artist who drew it.

Who is he?

What's the musical?

171Q. Two of the lyricists with whom Richard Rodgers collaborated each wrote a song that mentioned what was at one time Broadway's longest-running play.

The first lyricist wrote it with him in one of their earliest collaborations. The other lyricist wrote it *without* him, doing his own music to his own lyrics, in the decade after they had collaborated.

What's the play that each lyricist referenced?

What's the name of each song?

Who are the two lyricists?

172Q. Eugene O'Neill and Arthur Miller are considered two of America's greatest playwrights. They never collaborated, and their professional lives only overlapped by a few years.

But in a very strange way, there is a connection between the two.

What is it?

173Q. What musical that ran less than two weeks on Broadway had an opening number that only decades later became a Grammy-winning number one hit?

174Q. *Kiss Me, Kate; Kismet;* and *Man of La Mancha* all won multiple Tonys and sold plenty of cast albums too.

But what else do they have in common that almost—*almost*—applies to *My Fair Lady*, too?

175Q. When this musical began its tryout in Detroit, this song was the act 1 finale. It was later dropped from the original Broadway production, but it resurfaced in one of the show's many Broadway revivals—the most acclaimed one, in fact—as the act 2 opener.

What's the song?

What's the musical?

176Q. What do these shows have in common?

1) *Call Me Madam,* 2) *Mr. President,* 3) *Follies,* 4) *Godspell,* 5) *Starting Here, Starting Now,* 6) *Ain't Misbehavin',* 7) *A Class Act,* and 8) *Over Here!*

177Q. He wrote a novel and then coadapted it with a Broadway legend into a Tony-winning musical. His first name is a reasonably common one; for example, a performer who won a Best Actor in a Musical Tony in a twenty-first-century revival has it.

However, this writer spelled his name with an extra *s* at the end. The irony is that the performer who played the musical's hero also had that same name with the added *s*, but in this case, it was his last name.

What's the musical?

What was the first name of the co-bookwriter?

What was the last name of the musical's hero?

Who won the Best Actor in a Musical Tony in a twenty-first-century revival?

178Q. A nostalgic off-Broadway musical that opened in the late 1960s starred a performer whose leading lady wouldn't win the first of her Tonys until a dozen years after her understudy would win her first and only Tony (before leaving show business).

What's the musical?

Who was its star?

Who was the understudy?

What were the musicals that gave the star her first Tony and the understudy her only Tony?

179Q. From a certain song that each sings, we can tell that characters in *Guys and Dolls* and *Once Upon a Mattress* (both played by Tony-nominated performers)—as well as a character in *Hamilton* (played by a performer who indeed did win a Tony)—all spent their time in a certain activity.

Who are the characters?

What is the activity?

180Q. He's written four musicals that have run a substantial amount of time, but his first one, which started off-Broadway before moving uptown, is so famous that it has been produced by groups all around the world and was also made into a feature film.

In a twenty-first-century musical, it's being performed by a non-Equity cast in a Midwest state.

What is it?

What's the twenty-first-century musical?

181Q. Both Mary Martin and Pearl Bailey, when recording *Hello, Dolly!* changed one word in "So Long, Dearie" that Carol Channing had sung and Barbra Streisand would sing in the film version.

What's the original word?

What was the replacement word?

Why was the change made?

182Q. Two musicals were among the last to open in the 1960s. Both dealt with famous people. The subject of one—a man—had died many years earlier. The subject of the other—a woman—was then still alive.

Both musicals had as their titles their subjects' nicknames—nicknames of their first names, that is. But if you link his nickname in front of hers, you'll get the nickname of an actor who originated a lead role in a Neil Simon hit.

What was his nickname?

What was hers?

Who's the actor from the Simon play?

What's the name of the play?

183Q. A synonym for "twilight" set the wheels in motion for a successful twenty-first-century Best Musical Tony-nominee.

What is it?

184Q. In terms of the Best Musical Tony winners and losers that became films, what is interesting about the 1957–1958, 1962–1963, and 1975–1976 seasons?

185Q. What do these songs have in common?

1) "All about the Green" (*The Wedding Singer*), 2) "The Babylove Miracle Show" (*The Grass Harp*), 3) "Charity's Soliloquy" (*Sweet Charity*), and 4) "Standing on the Corner" (*The Most Happy Fella*).

186Q. A film that starred Steve McQueen was playing at the drive-in theater the teens in the film of *Grease* attended.

It also happens to be the title of as a Sondheim song that came, went, and returned to one of his musicals.

What is the name of the film and the song?

What's the musical?

187Q. For one of his musicals that wasn't commercially successful, Jerry Herman wrote a song with a title that was amazingly close to a song title that had been penned by Dorothy Fields for one of her musicals that had commercially succeeded.

What are the names of the two songs?

From what musicals did they come?

188Q. Rod, Nicky, Brian, Christmas Eve, Kate, and Princeton all live on Avenue Q. But many seasons earlier, a character from another musical was said to live one block south.

Who's this character?

In what musical does this character appear?

189Q. What musical, when produced in Germany, was called *Pinkelstadt?*

190Q. A hit musical from the very early 1950s that didn't win a Best Musical Tony could—considering the occupation of the leading lady—also be the name of a hit musical from the very late 1970s that also didn't win a Best Musical Tony.

(Hint: Each had its female lead win a Tony.)

What are the musicals?

191Q. What do these musicals have in common?

1) *Angel,* 2) *Dance A Little Closer,* 3) *Hot September,* 4) *The Most Happy Fella,* 5) *New Girl in Town,* 6) *Say Hello to Harvey,* 7) *Street Scene,* 8) *Yours Anne,* and 9) *Lovely Ladies, Kind Gentlemen.*

192Q. What statement made in a song in a 1981 quick flop musical was rebutted in 2000 by a song in a long-running hit musical?

193Q. He was a rather popular easy-listening recording star who became the leading man of a high profile 1960s musical that had some of Broadway's greatest creative names attached.

The revue in which his sister appeared opened about a year later; it was very low profile with names few if any on Broadway knew. And yet, it ran more than twice as long as her brother's eagerly anticipated musical. (That's show biz, folks!)

Who's the brother?

Who's his sister?

What were their respective shows?

194Q. Why are these musicals listed in this order?

1) *Sister Act,* 2) *A Tree Grows in Brooklyn,* 3) *It's So Nice to Be Civilized,* 4) *The Addams Family,* 5) *Pipe Dream,* 6) *Bring It On!,* and 7) *The Wedding Singer.*

195Q. There's a song from a very famous early 1960s Tony-winning musical that has four words in its title. You can hear the song on the original cast album, but not on the soundtrack, for it was dropped from the film version.

A little less than four years after that musical's Broadway opening, another musical opened on Broadway with a song that had the same four words in its title—except that the first word of the previous song was now the last word of the new song.

(Need an example? It's as if the first musical had a song called "Dance with Me, Henry" and the second musical had a song called "With Me Henry, Dance.")

The second musical lasted only a matter of months, despite the fact that one of its leads won a Tony. No original cast album was made of this flop. However, an actor who was in the film version of that aforementioned very famous early 1960s Tony-winning musical actually made a recording of the song from the flop. For that matter, so did Frank Sinatra.

What are the musicals?

What are the names of both four-word songs?

196Q. Although many people refer to the leading lady of *Gypsy* as Mama Rose, nowhere in the musical is she ever called that. But there's an even stronger argument to be made that Mama Rose is incorrect.

What is it?

197Q. When a Broadway musical has a title tune—a la "The Phantom of the Opera" or "The Sound of Music"—we expect it to be retained when the show is filmed. But one movie only retained the title's song's melody while omitting all its lyrics, but still made it a dance number.

What's the name of the title song, Broadway musical, and film?

198Q. One of musical theater's most illustrious musicals has a song that finished with a spoken sentence. It had six words that were followed by an orchestral note (or "button," if you will).

However, when the musical had its London premiere sixteen years later, the spoken sentence was replaced with "Well, I'll be damned!"

What's the song?

What's the musical?

What's the line that was replaced?

199Q. A famous musical says that its main character was born on October 28, but in the source material that inspired this hit, the character was established as having been born on February 29.

One of the words that describes that date is the first syllable of a word that appears late in the musical (but quite often in the source material).

Who's the character?

What's the musical?

What's the first syllable in question?

What does the character say in the musical?

200Q. An original cast album of a 1960s musical was originally issued with a cover that was primarily black but showed some prominent red.

However, when it was reissued five years later, it had a red cover with some prominent black.

What's the musical?

201Q. One of the most important people working on Broadway in the 1960s and 1970s was most celebrated for his work with two famous and acclaimed collaborators during the latter decade.

When these collaborators did their first musical in the 1980s, the person in question couldn't join them, because he'd died. Many lamented that the 1980s show suffered because he wasn't around to collaborate with them and the production sorely lacked his handiwork. The irony is that this flop musical opened precisely one year to the day after he'd died.

Who's this person?

Who were his two illustrious collaborators?

What's the musical that apparently needed his help?

202Q. Two different musicals written by the same much acclaimed composer-and-lyricist team each has a song that alludes to one of 1927's biggest headline-grabbing events.

One musical has had a smash-hit revival and the other was a flop that couldn't even reach a hundred performances.

What's the event?

What are the musicals?

What team wrote the scores?

203Q. In this famous songwriter's fourth-produced Broadway musical, a group of characters were known by a collective name. Take away the *s* at the end of that name, and you'll have the name that the main character gave a child in this same writer's fifth-produced Broadway musical (in which he *didn't* write both music and lyrics).

What's the name of the group?

In what musical do they appear?

What's the nickname given the child?

In what musical does he appear?

Who's the songwriter?

204Q. In the 1960s, a successful Broadway songwriting team took on a world-famous property and turned it into a musical, even though they weren't allowed to use many of the property's famous characters.

In the 1970s, this same team, when adapting another world-famous property, had the same restrictions imposed on them.

Who's the songwriting team?

What are the two properties they adapted?

What were the names of the two musicals?

What characters were they prevented from including?

205Q. A household novel of the nineteenth century became an enormously successful play some years later.

Its villain had a first and last name that would show up in a mid-twentieth-century musical—but this time, there was a preposition between the villain's first and last names.

What's the nineteenth-century novel and play?

What's the character's name?

What's the musical?

What was his expanded name?

206Q. A performer who won a Best Actress in a Play Tony in this century appeared at the same theater where she had made her first and only reviewed Broadway appearance as a performer almost a half-century earlier.

(The key word is "reviewed.")

Who is she?

207Q. A world-famous comedy has a five-word title. It was much later adapted into a not-famous off-Broadway musical that had a three-word title.

The last word of the famous play's title is almost but not quite spelled the same way as the first word of the musical's title.

What's the comedy?

What's the musical?

208Q. When you've seen or read *The Importance of Being Earnest,* have you ever noticed that those five words aren't quite the ones that end the play? Jack mentions "The *vital* importance of being earnest." Never is Oscar Wilde's actual title said in the play.

That brings to mind a Cole Porter song with a seven-word title. Nevertheless, those seven words aren't consecutively said in the song; an extra word comes between the fourth and fifth words.

What's the actual song title?

What's the extra word heard in the song?

209Q. Two Tony-nominated musicals began with the orchestra playing a song that had been dropped from the score before the Broadway opening.

One ran over a year; the other ran over two. Those original productions weren't the only time Broadway saw those musicals, although every subsequent production didn't offer the sets and costumes of the originals.

What are the musicals?

What are the names of the songs?

210Q. A musical that the writers gave a one-word title while they were creating it eventually appeared as a two-word title that started with the next letter of the alphabet. (It's as if *Evita* had been renamed *Funny Girl*).

The one-word title started with the same letter as the name of the theater where the show eventually played, although the theater has since been renamed.

What are the two names of the musical?

At what theater did it play?

211Q. What do these Tony-winners have in common?

1) Keene Curtis, 2) Randy Graff, 3) Anna Quayle, 4) Cyril Ritchard, 5) Victor Spinetti, 6) Scott Wise, and 7) Phil Silvers.

212Q. She appeared in a musical in the early 1960s where she supported one of the most famous TV superstars of all time. The song in which they duetted became a popular song that is still occasionally heard today.

Before this happened, however, she had been married to a composer who would later write a big 1960s Broadway hit that probably narrowly missed winning the Tony for Best Musical; he undoubtedly would have won his share of Best Original Score if the category had existed that year.

Who is she?

Who was her legendary costar?

Who was her ex-husband?

What musical did he compose?

213Q. When the original cast album of this now-famous and often revived—but *not* Tony-nominated—musical was released, its two stars were above the title.

Some years later, the recording was reissued with a new cover, but then the two stars had been joined above the title by a third, even though he'd only been fifth-billed on the original jacket.

What's the musical?

Who are the three stars?

214Q. In 1970, she opened in a musical in the spring; he opened in one in the fall. Both musicals closed on the same date, leaving them free for other work.

He eventually played the title character in a very successful TV series; some years later, she joined him on the show as his wife. In real life, she was the wife of the brother who wrote the lyrics to the musical that the actor did.

Who is she?

What musical did she do?

Who is he?

What musical did he do?

What's the TV series on which they appeared?

Who was her brother-in-law?

215Q. In a famous 1940s Broadway musical (a show that was even mentioned in an *Avenue Q* song), one man played the title character while the other was a dancer who had a tiny speaking part.

And yet, fewer than a dozen years later, both were in Hollywood codirecting a film that would become famous and beloved. Decades later, it would become a Broadway musical.

Who are the two men?

What was the musical in which they both performed?

What was the film that they codirected?

216Q. Two composers and one lyricist wrote a song that years later became the title song of a Tony-winning jukebox musical.

They originally described it as having a "Tempo de Naughty Groovy." The description has since been changed to "Moderately," but the song title and the musical's title remain the same.

What are they?

217Q. What major character in a Rodgers and Hammerstein hit has the fewest lines?

218Q. These two names in two different musicals aren't quite spelled the same, but they certainly sound the same.

One is the maiden name of a character who still uses it between her first and married name; she appeared in a Tony-winning musical that's had more than one Broadway revival.

The other is the actual surname of a performer who won Best Actress in a Musical in a Tony-winning Best Musical.

What's the name of each woman?

What musicals are referenced here?

219Q. She is one of the most famous pop singers of the late twentieth century. Although she once brought a glorified concert to the Palace Theatre, no one would associate her first and foremost with Broadway.

And yet, she and her two well-known backup singers did make a studio cast album of a much-admired, Tony-nominated score. The irony is that the musical in question opened on this singer's twentieth birthday.

Who is she?

What's the musical?

220Q. When they made a movie together in the 1950s, the performer we'll call A was the top-billed star while the performer we'll call B was third-billed.

However, in the following decade, Performer B was the star of a wildly successful Broadway musical; once she left, Performer A was brought in as her successor.

Who were the two performers?

What was the hit musical?

What was the less successful film?

221Q. There was a time when four musicals were the longest-running tenants at their respective theaters—all of which had Rodgers and Hammerstein's names on their *Playbill* title pages.

What were the four musicals that once set these long-run records?

What were the four theaters?

222Q. In one of his films (which became a stage musical that closed in California), Frank Sinatra sang a song that was nominated for an Academy Award.

In it, he sang a certain word ten times—a word that just happens to be the name of a famous Broadway musical. What's more, the body of this song includes three words that are found in the opening number of that same stage musical.

What's the film?

What's the song?

What's the repeated word that became the name of a famous musical?

What are the three words that are found in the musical's opening number?

223Q. What Sondheim song from a 1970s musical is also the name of a fictional musical that's in a genuine hit Broadway musical of the 1980s?

224Q. What do these shows have in common?

1) *Kwamina,* 2) *1776,* 3) *Lady Day at Emerson's Bar & Grill,* 4) *La Cage aux Folles,* 5) *Aspects of Love,* and 6) *In the Heights.*

225Q. What 1960s Tony-nominated musical—the first but hardly the last Tony-nominated musical that this composer-lyricist would have—included a lyric that referenced not one but *two* Rodgers and Hammerstein songs in one line?

(Seriously: Out of eight words, five were originally Hammerstein's.)

What's the song?

What's the musical?

What's the composer-lyricist's name?

226Q. Comparatively speaking, musicals don't have many songs that begin with the letter J. However, one Tony season, everyone who won a Tony in a musical category was in a show that had a song that began with the letter J.

In what Tony season did this happen?

What are the three musicals?
What are the three songs?

227Q. At some point during the game of Monopoly, you'd most likely have the chance to sing the title of an appropriate Rodgers and Hart song from one of their 1930s hits.

What's the song?
What's the musical?

228Q. When this musical received its off-Broadway recording, this song was the sixteenth cut on the cast album. When the musical moved to Broadway (after a stop somewhere else), this song became the show's opening number.

What's the song?
What's the show?

229Q. For the 1982 revue *Upstairs at O'Neal's,* Martin Charnin wrote a song called "Stools." It stated, "You can't do a revue without stools" before admitting that "you can do a revue without taste. I know of one that's been running for years."

To what revue was he referring?

230Q. The 1970 British musical *Sing a Rude Song* has one song that mentions what would be the title character of a Tony-winning musical by the end of the decade.

The character had absolutely nothing to do with the plot of *Sing a Rude Song,* but no one would dispute that if we used the adjective "rude" for his last solo in act 1, we'd be substantially understating the case.

Who is he?

231Q. An eighteenth-century novel has a title extraordinarily close to a nineteenth-century play. In fact, there's only one letter difference. That novel became a twentieth-century musical with the same title.

What's the novel?

What's the play?
What's the musical?

232Q. A very minor character in a 1950s Tony-nominated musical has the same surname of a much more important character in a 1980s Tony-nominated musical. The performer who played him won a Best Featured Actor in a Musical Tony.

What's the surname?
What are the musicals?
Who won the Tony?

233Q. What do these musicals have in common?

1) *Hair,* 2) *Hamilton,* 3) *Legs Diamond,* 4) *I'm Getting My Act Together and Taking It on the Road,* 5) *Passing Strange,* 6) *Stop the World—I Want to Get Off,* and 7) *The Roar of the Greasepaint—The Smell of the Crowd.*

234Q. A Best Actress in a Musical Tony-winner, in her Tony-winning musical (that rather quickly closed after she left), was the first to use the words "rock and roll" in a musical theater song.

What's the lyric?
What's the song?
What's the musical?
Who sang it?

235Q. What do these songs have in common?

1) "I Don't Remember Christmas" (*Starting Here, Starting Now*), 2) "Just the Crust" (*Skyscraper*), 3) "Who Knows What Might Have Been?" (*Subways Are for Sleeping*), and 4) "Opening Doors" (*Merrily We Roll Along*).

236Q. In a Pulitzer Prize–winning musical, its secondary male lead repeated his role in its film version. He is also mentioned in a song from a 1965–1966 Tony-nominated musical.

Who's the star?

What's the song?

What are the two musicals?

237Q. In the same year, this performer was in not one but two musicals that mentioned the dance with which the nation was then obsessed.

In the first of the two musicals, she simply mentioned the dance in dialogue in the middle of a song. In the second, she actually sang an entire song about this dance.

Who's the performer?

What were the songs?

What were the musicals?

238Q. What's the longest word to be found in any musical theater song?

239Q. She was cast as one of the leads in what would become a Rodgers and Hammerstein hit. He landed a small role in the same production.

Both happened to have the same last name, one that has three syllables in it. He chose to change it—not because he necessarily wanted to, but because he thought she, in the more important role, should be the one to have it.

So he cut the final two syllables of his name and retained only the first one, although he then decided to spell that first syllable differently. When the film was made, the stage star wasn't in it, but he was—and in a substantially better role.

Who was she?

Who was he?

What was the stage show and film?

240Q. What name of a fictional musical, mentioned in act 2 of a quick flop that has nevertheless endured, originally had the subtitle *The Barbara Hutton Story?*

241Q. This legendary composer-lyricist won one and only one Best Score Tony. The surname by which the world knows him is *not* the surname he had at birth; he changed it.

But his *real* surname is an anagram of the surname of an actress who appeared in a musical that same season that virtually everyone thinks *should* have won Best Score.

Who's the composer-lyricist?

What's his real surname?

What's the anagrammed surname of the actress?

In what musical did she appear that has passed the test of time as the better score?

242Q. We've all been told that the best musical theater songs move the action forward. But a Tony-winning musical had a comedy song in its second act that didn't; after another song was sung, that comedy song was reprised, but it *still* didn't move the action forward.

However, when this musical was made into a film, the lyricist rewrote the song to include two characters who were in the show on Broadway, yes, but weren't in the number. In the film, the song now moved the action forward.

What's the song?

What's the musical?

Who are the two characters who sang in the film?

How did the song move the action forward?

243Q. Five of the six Rodgers and Hammerstein film musicals based on their hit Broadway shows had something in common. *Carousel* is the exception for three reasons.

What are they?

244Q. For the first two productions of this hit musical, a character seen only in the first scene (and who didn't say a word) wasn't given a name in the script or the *Playbill;* instead, he was named for what he wore—although the title character of the musical *did* say the character's nickname.

Finally, in the musical's second revival, the script and *Playbill* listed the character by his nickname.

What's the musical?

Who's the title character?

What's the nickname of the other character?

What did he wear that provided the description in the script and *Playbill?*

245Q. A Tony-winning musical had one noun in its title. Some years before it opened, however, Sondheim had written a song that used that same word as a preposition.

No, the actual preposition wouldn't be spelled the way Sondheim spelled it, but he was filtering it through another language.

What's the musical?

What's the Sondheim song?

What's the musical from which it came?

246Q. Any musical that opens downtown hopes to move uptown. This one did after receiving great reviews and many awards.

But after it moved uptown, it eventually moved downtown again, although to a different theater from its first downtown theater.

Then it eventually moved uptown again, although to yet *another* theater.

(Some hints: One of those theaters doesn't exist anymore; one has a different name; and the two others have been repurposed.)

What's this musical?

247Q. A musical from the 1950s that won no Tonys at all—as well as a musical from the 1970s that won quite a few—both mention one mythical character, one nineteenth-century person known for his fashion sense, and one Broadway and film star of many decades ago.

What are the musicals?

In what three songs are these three people named?

248Q. Sheldon Harnick, in his 1959 musical *Fiorello!*, had his political candidate in "The Name's La Guardia" sing "Well, there's a double 'M' in Tammany and a double 'L' in gall."

Two consecutive words in that line actually became the title of a later Harnick song, although one of those words is a homonym.

Remember homonyms from your grammar school days? They're words that sound the same but are spelled differently—like see, *s-e-e*, meaning vision, and sea, *s-e-a*, meaning a body of water.

What's the song?

From what musical does it come?

249Q. Both Lorenz Hart and Cole Porter made a rhyme that purposely mispronounced a word in a most famous Oscar-winning film.

But they weren't just cheating to make a rhyme; the mispronunciation had become an idiom over the years, and theatergoers had undoubtedly heard it before they'd entered the theater.

What are the songs?

What are the lyrics?

What's the Oscar-winning film?

250Q. She never appeared on Broadway, but she did make movies of three Broadway hits as well as one Broadway flop.

She had three husbands, and although she didn't take the last name of the third, had she done so, she would have then had the name of one of Broadway's first musical theater superstars.

Who are these two women?

251Q. It opened on the same date that *Oklahoma!* did—only many years later. It wasn't a musical, and it only ran sixteen performances off-Broadway. But its cast included a woman who would win a Best

Featured Actress in a Play Tony only a year after the play in question had closed.

More to the point—if this play hadn't been produced and she and one of the coproducers hadn't met, someone else would have won an Oscar thirty years later.

What's the play?

Who won the Tony?

Who was the coproducer?

Who won the Oscar three decades later?

252Q. *Aladdin* has "Arabian Nights." *Irene* has "An Irish Girl." *A Day in Hollywood* has "Japanese Sandman."

But a very famous Tony-winning musical has three songs, each of which mentions the name of a different nationality. When the film version was made, however, all three songs were dropped.

What's the musical?

What are the songs?

253Q. A performer in the original cast of a Rodgers and Hammerstein musical had an unusual name. Her first name was the name of a city and her second name was not only the name of one of the United States, but the actual state in which this city can be found.

Who had this odd name?

In what Rodgers and Hammerstein musical could we have found her?

254Q. These songs have something in common and are listed in this order for a reason.

1) "Puttin' on the Ritz" (*Young Frankenstein*), 2) "At the Fountain" (*Sweet Smell of Success*), 3) "One Night in Bangkok" (*Chess*), 4) "Give Them What They Want" (*Dirty Rotten Scoundrels*), 5) "Masculinity" (*La Cage aux Folles*), 6) "But Alive" (*Applause*), and 7) "Unworthy of Your Love" (*Assassins*).

255Q. Why are the years representing the Best Musical Tony-winners listed in this order?

1) 1953–1954, 2) 1949–1950, 3) 1948–1949, 4) 1951–1952, and 5) 1985–1986.

256Q. A character in a late 1980s musical had a German name. If you translate it into English, you'll get the name of an early Kander and Ebb song.

What's the name of the character?

What's the English translation and name of the song?

What are the musicals?

257Q. Why are these musicals' names in this specific order?

1) *The Roar of the Greasepaint—The Smell of the Crowd*, 2) *Into the Woods*, 3) *Rags*, 4) *Pacific Overtures*, 5) *Minnie's Boys*, 6) *Damn Yankees*, 7) *Camelot*, 8) *She Loves Me*, 9) *42nd Street*, 10) *Bloody Bloody Andrew Jackson*, 11) *Merrily We Roll Along*, 12) *The Who's Tommy*, 13) *Newsies*, and 14) *Let's Face It*.

258Q. He wrote the music and lyrics for a Tony-winning musical. Ironically, his name can *almost* be found in the names of two of the show's characters. His first name was the surname of one character; his last name includes the first name of another character.

Who is he?

Who are the characters?

What's the musical?

259Q. A character in a 1980s musical estimated that a 1960s musical would run at least 7,434 performances. Granted, the musical for which he had high hopes was a mythical one, but the other three were for real.

Explain.

260Q. Two writers with the same three initials—and the same last name—had a marked influence on a world-famous Broadway musical.

One provided the inspiration for the show. The other made his mark eleven months after the original Broadway production had closed—and long after the Tony committee had denied it a Best Musical nomination.

What's the musical?

Who are the two writers?

How did they influence the musical?

261Q. One of Stephen Sondheim's songs starts with a musical phrase that you can hear in the overture of *Song of Norway*. It's also heard in the act 1 finale of a Pulitzer Prize–winning musical.

What's the Sondheim song?

What's the *Song of Norway* song?

What's the Pulitzer Prize–winning musical?

262Q. In 1972, a song from a very successful off-Broadway show was released as a 45 rpm single record and reached as high as number thirteen on the charts.

It was *not* a cover recording made by a then-popular group, but was actually taken from the show's very successful original album. However, the name attributed to the "group" was simply the name of the musical.

What's the name of the song?

What's the name of the musical?

263Q. What do these songs have in common?

1) "Cabaret" (*Cabaret*), 2) "The Worst Pies in London" (*Sweeney Todd*), 3) "They're Playing Our Song" (*They're Playing Our Song*), 4) "The Big Dollhouse" (*Hairspray*), 5) "My Unfortunate Erection" (*The 25th Annual Putnam County Spelling Bee*), and 6) "Colored Lights" (*The Rink*).

264Q. Fewer than four dozen people in the entire history of the United States have done this job. George M. Cohan, Len Cariou, and Dee Hoty once played characters who have.

What's the job?

In what shows did they do it?

265Q. Before this musical began its pre-Broadway tryout, one of its songs was recorded by a best-selling singer.

But en route to Broadway, the lyricist decided to scrap that lyric and instead create a title song for the show. The irony is that when the film version was made, her second set of lyrics was retained but the composer gave it a new melody.

What's the musical (and therefore the name of the title song)?

What was the song originally titled?

Who recorded it before Broadway?

266Q. Vera Charles in *Mame* sang that "the man in the moon is a lady." But an even more famous musical from the previous decade (that also lost the Best Musical Tony) had a young man make the same observation, although in dialogue.

What's that musical?

Which character said it?

267Q. How did a Lerner and Loewe song wind up in a play that had music by Jule Styne and lyrics by Betty Comden and Adolph Green?

268Q. The window card of this famous star's second and final musical simply had a logo of orange circles that included a black-and-white picture of her from head to toe.

But the photograph used wasn't one that came from this musical, but from a big hit show she had done seven years earlier—one for which she won a Best Actress in a Musical Tony.

Who is she?

What's the first musical?

What's the second?

269Q. In the 1960s, he was nominated for a Grammy for a Tony-winning musical for which he didn't write a word. In the 1970s, he won a Tony for a musical for which he wrote hundreds of words.

Who is he?

What are the musicals?

270Q. On December 28, 1982, a playwright who'd eventually have more than a dozen Broadway productions saw his first Broadway play begin previews at the theater that sat next to a theater where a different playwright's one and only Broadway attraction was appearing.

If you stood in front of the theaters and looked at both marquees, you might be reminded of a famous candy concoction that is still being manufactured today.

Explain.

271Q. A "May-December romance" refers to a relationship between a young person and an older one. Name the musical that actually opened in May and closed in December that involved just such a situation.

(Hint: Its songwriter had already contributed the score for one Tony-winning Best Musical and would eventually have another.)

272Q. He almost always cowrote plays, many of which became films. However, the one that opened on Broadway with a seventy-six-year-old actress in the lead was reconceived as a film in which a thirty-five-year-old actress assumed the role.

Coincidentally, both actresses had the same initials.

Who was the playwright?

What's the play?

Who were the two actresses?

273Q. Under what circumstances could we say that a song from *Damn Yankees* and one from *The Fantasticks* could respectively be called "Shoeless Fire from Hannibal, Mo" and "Soon It's Gonna Tess"?

274Q. The first hit this team had—but certainly not the last—originally had an eight-letter title. Eventually, the bookwriter-lyricist decided to add one letter, which he put in front of the eight letters, making a nine-letter title.

    (Hint: That extra letter is a homonym for a type of insect.)

    What was the musical's first name?

    What was it eventually called?

275Q. In Michael Stewart's book for *Hello, Dolly!* he had his title character mention a nineteenth-century stage star who turned up as an actual character in one of his later shows.

    Who is this former luminary?

    In what Stewart musical does she actually appear?

276Q. We're looking for the name of a musical with a score by two Broadway legends. It was set in Italy, and its title song colloquially alludes to a piece by an Austrian composer.

    What's the musical and its title song?

    Who wrote the score?

    What's the allusion to the Austrian composer's work?

    Who was he?

277Q. What do these musicals have in common?

    1) *Charlie and Algernon,* 2) *Gypsy,* 3) *Fade Out—Fade In,* 4) *Happy Hunting,* 5) *Legally Blonde,* and 6) *Lovely Ladies, Kind Gentlemen.*

278Q. Two Best Musical Tony-winners that won their prizes nine years apart both start their overtures in the same but most atypical way.

    Explain why.

    Name the musicals.

279Q. What do these songs have in common?

1) "America" (*West Side Story*), 2) "Meat and Potatoes" (*Mr. President*), 3) "When You're Home" (*In the Heights*), 4) "An English Teacher" (*Bye Bye Birdie*), and 5) "The House We Live In" (*Grey Gardens*).

280Q. One of Stephen Sondheim's most famous lyrics—in a show for which he wrote only lyrics—contains two lines that became the title of a 1970s supper club revue.

It has received both American and British cast albums. Its title song was recorded by a very famous recording artist.

What are the two lines?

What's the show?

Who recorded the song?

281Q. The same opening number, although differently orchestrated, opened different musicals in 1952, 1956, 1962, and 1968.

What's the name of the song?

What are the names of the four shows?

282Q. It closed as one of the fifteen longest-running plays in Broadway history. Its leading lady was acclaimed and Tony-nominated for what she'd brought to it. However, when the film version was made, she only got to appear in a third of it.

What's the name of the play?

Who's the actress?

283Q. What do these songs have in common?

1) "When the Idle Poor Become the Idle Rich" (*Finian's Rainbow*), 2) "Where Is the Life That Late I Led?" (*Kiss Me, Kate*), 3) "The Seven Deadly Virtues" (*Camelot*), 4) "Hurry! It's Lovely Up Here!" (*On a Clear Day You Can See Forever*), 5) "The Year of the Child" (*Falsettos*), 6) "Paula" (*The Goodbye Girl*), 7) "No One Mourns the Wicked" (*Wicked*), and 8) "The 'I Love You' Song" (*The 25th Annual Putnam County Spelling Bee*).

284Q. What one musical has caused Sondheim's musicals to lose a Tony on three separate occasions?

285Q. What performer who appeared in 76 of *Green Acres*'s 170 episodes—and yet never received billing—also appeared in the film version of *1776?*

286Q. An eleven o'clock number in a long-running revival of a Broadway musical includes a two-line lyric that is relevant to a famous twenty-first-century revival of a Sondheim musical.

What's the lyric?

What song and musical it is from?

On what Sondheim show does it just happen to comment—not that it set out to do that?

287Q. In his first Broadway musical, he wrote for a female character whose goal was exactly the same as the female character for his second Broadway musical.

However, in the first (a long-running money-loser) she *sings* about what she wants—while in the second (a long-running smash hit) she instead has a speech about what she wants.

Who's the writer?

What are the two musicals?

What's the song?

Describe the speech.

288Q. Songs are the reason that these musicals have been placed in this order.

1) *A Christmas Story,* 2) *Hands Up,* 3) *The Visit,* 4) *Sweeney Todd,* 5) *Spring Awakening,* 6) *Sophisticated Ladies,* and 7) *Shenandoah.*

289Q. He was nominated for five Tonys over a career that also included an Oscar win for Best Song. And yet, his score for a musical that closed out of town remains the least successful musical version of a Pulitzer Prize–winning play.

Who is he?

What's the Pulitzer Prize–winning play?

What was the name of its musical adaptation?

290Q. A musical from 1918 has a three-word title as well as a score by a very famous composer-lyricist who eventually won a Best Score Tony for a much later show. The musical's first two words are identical, and just happen to be the nickname of a very famous lyricist.

What's the musical?

Who wrote its score?

Who's the lyricist?

291Q. What do these items have in common?

1) a Tony-winning hit from this century, 2) an a cappella off-Broadway musical from last century, and 3) a Jerry Herman song.

292Q. If Michael Bennett had stayed with his first impulse, the three performers who each won a Tony for *A Chorus Line* would have had something in common.

Explain.

293Q. *Dream,* a 1997 revue of songs by lyricist and sometimes composer Johnny Mercer, played Broadway. Although songs from his 1946 musical *St. Louis Woman* were included, there were none from his not-too-long-running musical from the 1940s, and none from his long-running hit in the 1950s (which even received a movie version).

Each of them had the same word in their titles, each of which was a contraction—meaning a word that includes an apostrophe replacing a letter or letters in a word.

What's the name of the not-too-long-running musical from the 1940s?

What's the name of the long-running hit from the 1950s?

294Q. A famous Republican politician wrote a book and chose as his title the name of a song from a Pulitzer Prize–winning musical. As of this writing, he's never won a major award—but a performer who has the same name as the author played a character who indeed did win one (well, at least one that he thought was major).

What are the names of both the politician and the actor?

What's the name of the politician's book?

What character won "the major award"?

295Q. In 2022, as he was going to his audition in hopes of landing a certain role in an upcoming Broadway revival, this performer with a Roman numeral after his name might well have been singing a famous song from a famous 1920s musical.

Who is he?

What's the revival for which he auditioned (successfully, in fact)?

What's the song that would have been apt for him to sing?

From what musical does it come?

296Q. What do these musicals, all of which received at least one Tony nomination, otherwise have in common?

1) *The Best Little Whorehouse Goes Public,* 2) *Crazy for You,* 3) *Saturday Night Fever,* 4) *The Scarlet Pimpernel,* 5) *Seussical,* 6) *Steel Pier,* 7) *Thoroughly Modern Millie,* and 8) *Victor/Victoria.*

297Q. A show that closed some months shy of becoming Broadway's longest-running musical shuttered ten years to the *day* of the opening of a show that *did* become Broadway's longest-running musical.

What are the two shows?

298Q. Comparatively few musicals have had titles that include *&*—an ampersand, as it's called. But someone connected with two of them received a total of four Tony nominations.

Who was the nominee?

What were the musicals?

299Q. The title of a song in a 1960s Best Score Tony-winner is the name of a state. Ironically, that state was admitted to the union 142 years to the day before the musical opened.

What's the name of the state and song?

What's the musical?

300Q. A 1980s nightclub revue includes a song that mentions *Fiddler on the Roof, Little Shop of Horrors, Mata Hari, One Mo' Time, 1600 Pennsylvania Avenue, Via Galactica,* and *Oh, Brother!*

What is it?

301Q. A man's nickname that was the title character of a failed musical version of a famous and much admired play is also the name of a young woman in a popular song that decades later wound up in a jukebox musical.

What's the name of the song?

From what musicals do they come?

302Q. Two characters in Tony-winning musicals of successive seasons were played by leading performers who won Tonys themselves. The characters had the same initials as well as a similar outlook toward women.

Who are they?

What were their musicals?

What song best illustrates each character's outlook?

303Q. A wildly successful movie musical of a wildly successful Broadway musical had four leads who averaged twenty-eight years in age.

What was the property?

Who were the four performers?

Why was their age a potential problem?

304Q. Many Tony-winning musicals have two distinctly different couples in love. One is often older and more serious than the younger couple. Usually, you'll hear either the male or female—of both couples—say "I love you!" in the show. But in this Tony-winning musical, "I love you!" is said by a father to another man.

What's the musical?

Who says it to whom?

305Q. When this musical opened off-Broadway, it had a scene set on a Friday in late November that contained only a snatch of a song. When it came on Broadway more than a dozen years later, it had a full song added to that scene.

What was the musical?

What was the new song?

306Q. A song that appeared in a 1980s jukebox musical is also the name of a song that a very famous entertainer sang in a one-person show at a Broadway theater that's almost literally (but not quite) on Broadway.

The title of the song could have been the title of a song in a Mary Martin vehicle. (The entire lyric of the song wouldn't be apt, no—but the title would.)

What's the song?

What's the jukebox musical?

Who's the famous entertainer who sang it near Broadway?

What's the Mary Martin vehicle?

307Q. It really wasn't a scandal when Jerry Bock and Sheldon Harnick decided that Jerome Coopersmith's book for their upcoming musical of *The Diary of Adam and Eve* wasn't quite what they hoped for and parted company with him.

However, if we *chose* to call it a scandal, we could make it into a term by using a famous suffix that's often applied to a scandal. This new term would also be the name of a character that was played by a performer who'd won a Best Actor in a Musical Tony a decade earlier.

What's the character?

Who played him?

From what musical did he come?

What Bock and Harnick musical was involved?

308Q. He was nominated as Best Actor in a Musical and she was nominated as Best Actress in a Musical for the same show. Neither of them won, but each had already won a Tony.

And yet, add up all their songs, and you'll find they had less to sing than two people who are heard more often on the original cast album—two people, in fact, who had never before appeared on Broadway and never would again. (The two nominees, however, would make other Broadway appearances.)

What's the musical?

Who are the two stars?

(You needn't name the two unknowns unless you really want to.)

309Q. In the first film version of a world-famous musical, a group of young men whistle a famous nineteenth-century song that wasn't originally written for a musical. However, this vintage song happens to have the same title as a song that *was* written specifically for this musical.

What's the name of both songs?

What's the musical?

310Q. Musicals are famous for title songs. What Tony-winning musical has a title song only in a manner of speaking—because the show's title is in another language. The English translation of the word is the name of the show's third song.

What's the show's title?

What's the name of the song?

311Q. Those who weren't yet alive in the 1970s—and who listen to a Kander and Ebb musical from that decade—may infer a name mentioned in one of its songs refers to a very famous Charles Dickens character.

It does not, although the name is identical to the one Dickens chose.

What's the identical name?

To whom does it refer?

In what song and musical does it occur?

312Q. In a manner of speaking—loosely speaking (*very* loosely speaking)—what songs in *A Little Night Music* could be said to have reprises?

313Q. He appeared on Broadway in a comedy that had the same title as the name of a song in a Sondheim musical in which he'd starred ten years earlier. Although he's a multiple Tony-winner, he did not win for either of these productions.

Who's the star?

What's the name of the comedy?

What's the name of the song?

From what musical does it come?

314Q. The Theatre World books that were once published annually would list song titles for every musical of the season.

In one edition, it claimed that a certain song was called "Goodbye, Failure, Goodbye." According to the cast album, the studio cast album, and the *Playbill,* that's not the song's official title.

What is?

From what musical does it come?

315Q. Remember in high school math when you had to solve those analogy problems that said 3 is to 6 as 6 is to . . . and the answer was 12?

Here's a musical theater–centric one: Charles Strouse is to Frank Wildhorn as Henry Mancini is to whom?

316Q. The first name of a legendary two-time Tony-winner is pronounced the same (but not spelled the same) as the since-razed venue that was the second stop for an off-Broadway musical that would eventually move to Broadway as its third stop, where it would run for years.
  What are the homonyms?
  What's the name of the musical?

317Q. What do these musicals have in common?
  1) *Avenue Q,* 2) *Carnival,* 3) *Guys and Dolls,* 4) *Seussical,* and 5) *SpongeBob SquarePants.*

318Q. What character in *A Funny Thing Happened on the Way to the Forum* is scheduled to play Medea later that week?

319Q. A famous TV series of this century was later parodied as an off-Broadway stage musical. It has the same name as a play that closed in previews, despite being staged by one of the most famous directors (and, for that matter, choreographers) in Broadway history.
  What is the name of the series and the musical?
  Who was the famous director who couldn't make it a hit?

320Q. He appeared on two original cast albums on which a yawn is heard. The first yawn wasn't done by him, but by the star of the show who was making her illustrious Broadway debut. On the later album, however, he yawned during his only solo in the show.
  Who is he?
  What are the two musicals?
  What's the name of his solo?
  Who was the earlier yawner?

321Q. As a composer, he was a one-hit wonder, with one Best Musical and Best Score to his credit. His next musical closed in Philadelphia. As for the one after that, he and everyone connected with it had a problem settling on a title, for it changed titles twice en route to Broadway.

What was the musical?

What were the titles?

Who was the composer?

What was his sole hit?

322Q. On what original cast album—well, a 99 and 44/100 percent original cast album—can you hear a woman who won one competitive Tony (but not for this musical), a man who won a few Emmys, and a man who won many Tonys, many Grammys, an Oscar, and a Pulitzer Prize?

PART THREE

QUESTIONS

I'M A GENIUS GENIUS

323Q. What title of a Bob Merrill musical would have been a terribly inaccurate name for a Richard Rodgers musical that was produced nine years after Merrill's?

324Q. What do these songs have in common?

1) "Take Back Your Mink" (*Guys and Dolls*), 2) "Diamonds Are a Girl's Best Friend" (*Gentlemen Prefer Blondes*), 3) "Six Months out of Every Year" (*Damn Yankees*), 4) "A Summer in Ohio" (*The Last 5 Years*), 5) "For Now" (*Avenue Q*), and most especially 6) "Standing on the Corner" (*The Most Happy Fella*).

325Q. In *The Full Monty,* when Jerry and Dave pull Malcolm out of the car that's filling up with carbon monoxide, what line from a show that won both the Best Musical Tony and a Pulitzer Prize could they have said to him?

326Q. The four songs from these musicals mention four famous plays.

What are they?

Why are they in this order? 1) A song in a Rodgers and Hart musical, 2) It's mentioned within a duet in Comden and Green's first musical, 3) It appears in a now-famous song that Stephen Sondheim wrote during the Boston tryout of one of his musicals, and 4) It can be found in the song title of a Harold Rome musical.

327Q. *Porgy and Bess* was greatly inspired by a person associated with the play that preceded it. But one might inadvertently—and incorrectly—also associate this individual with a Rodgers and Hammerstein classic.

Who's the person?

Why would the mistake be made?

328Q. What Rodgers and Hart musical was revived virtually a quarter century after its debut but only after having its book revised by a writer who was almost exclusively working as a lyricist?

(Hint: He'd recently won a Tony for his lyrics in a Best Score.)

329Q. Three musicals that start with the letter *M*—*My Fair Lady, Man of La Mancha,* and *Molly*—all have something else in common.

What?

330Q. The first songs sung by Horace Vandergelder in *Hello, Dolly!* and Georgina Franklin in *Hallelujah, Baby!* show these uneducated characters seeming out of character in using the same grammatically precise expression.

What is the expression?

What are the songs?

331Q. What Tony-winning musical employed four singers who were collectively known by the same name as a New York sports team?

332Q. What do the Broadway theaters Lyceum, Lyric, Palace, and Sondheim have in common?

333Q. What musical had an original cast that had appeared in eighty-eight different shows in which they gave a total of 37,095 performances?

334Q. A 1950s musical that has been much produced in amateur theater—but had an unsuccessful Broadway revival in the 1990s— has a dance for which no lyrics were written, but its title mentions a certain nationality.

When it was first adapted for TV, the dance retained that nationality, but when it was *next* adapted for TV, the nationality was changed.

What's the musical?

What's the name of each dance?

335Q. What do these shows have in common?

1) *The Best Little Whorehouse in Texas,* 2) *My Fair Lady,* 3) *The Rocky Horror Show,* 4) *Spongebob Squarepants,* and 5) *Urinetown.*

336Q. In the 1950s, an Oscar-nominated film version of a famous stage comedy listed this fictional actor among the ones who would be in the fictional play *Midsummer Madness.*

In the 1960s, the screenwriters of that film gave that name to the leading man of their original musical.

(Hint: His previous Broadway appearance saw him win a Best Featured Actor in a Musical Tony.)

What was the film of the famous play?

What was the character's name?

Who played him in the later musical?

For what performance did he win a Tony?

337Q. What do these musicals have in common?

1) a legendary, world-famous musical from the 1940s, 2) a 1950s musical that won two of theater's most prestigious awards, 3) a long-running show from the 1960s, 4) a one-performance flop from the early 1970s, 5) a 1980s African musical that ran nearly a year and a

half, and 6) a 1990s musical version of *Twelfth Night* that lasted fifty-two nights.

338Q. When he first started producing, he used his full first name, middle initial, and last name. As the years went on, he shortened his first name to a nickname, and dropped his middle initial.

Take the two remaining words of the name by which he was most known, reverse them, and you'll get the name of a famous Shakespearean character.

Who are they?

In what plays does the character appear?

339Q. The kids in *You're a Good Man, Charlie Brown* wouldn't seem to have anything in common with Lily Garland in *On the Twentieth Century*. Nevertheless, all of them do have some sort of involvement with a famous fictional character.

Who is it?

340Q. What musical nominated for five Tonys (and won one) includes these lines?

"On the shore dimly seen through the mists of the deep where the foe's haughty host in dread silence reposes. What is that which the breeze, o'er the towering steep, as it fitfully blows, half conceals, half discloses."

341Q. A year after one actor had received an Oscar nomination, an actress who had been in a musical with him got one as well.

Neither he nor she won, but these nominations had to be career highlights considering that both had appeared in a famous Tony-winning musical in which neither sang a note.

Who are they?

For what were their Oscar nominations?

What was the musical in which both appeared?

342Q. A person we'll call Performer A received a Best Actress in a Musical Tony in a show that won a Best Musical Tony, too.

When Performer A left that show, a person we'll call Performer B took over—someone who two years earlier had won a Best Actress in a Musical Tony.

Performer A eventually did a movie musical and performed a song whose title just happens to be the same as the name of the first Broadway musical—a quick flop—in which Performer B made her Broadway debut.

Who are the performers?

What are the musicals?

What's the song?

343Q. There's a great eleven o'clock number in a 1960s Broadway musical that has three words in its title.

The first two of those words are the same two words of the three-word title of a *very* short-running 1970s Broadway musical.

The irony is that the third word of the flop's title—a proper name of someone known only by one name and no surname—eventually turns up in the lyric of that eleven o'clock number.

What's the song?

From what musical does it come?

What's the name of the short-running 1970s flop?

344Q. What do these performers have in common?

1) Maria Chapa, 2) Veanne Cox, 3) Linda Hart, and 4) Phyllis Newman.

345Q. Take the name of a not-so-famous Steven Spielberg movie. Do a little switching within the title, and you'll come up with the name of a famous composer-lyricist's final musical that closed out of town.

346Q. He was the costar in a 1950s musical in which he warred with his much more famous costar. His son is mentioned in a lyric of a twenty-first-century Tony-nominated Best Musical.

Who are the father and son?

In what musical did the father appear?

In what song and in what musical was the son mentioned?

347Q. "Lyricists love cleverness," William Goldman wrote in his 1969 landmark book, *The Season.* As exhibit A, he offered "*Uppity* rhyming with *cup of tea.*"

Indeed, during the season that Goldman covered (1967–1968) there was one musical in which *uppity* was rhymed with *cup of tea.*

What was the line?

What was the name of the song?

What was the name of the musical?

348Q. A famous costume designer was fired from a 1950s musical that eventually won a Best Musical Tony without her. Nevertheless, she was hired for the musical's film version and received an Oscar nomination for it.

Who is she?

What was the property?

349Q. In her first starring role in a hit musical, she simply said the expression "Go to hell." More than twenty years later, in her last starring role in a hit musical—one that ran virtually as long—she angrily sang "Go to hell!" along with her famous costar.

The irony is that in one of her most famous roles, she would have never said "Go to hell!"

Who is she?

What were the musicals?

What were the circumstances that caused her to use the expression?

350Q. What does Roger De Bris have in common with the actress who played the lead in a 2002 musical revival—the fourth revival this musical has had on Broadway?

351Q. What do these musicals have in common?

1) *The Baker's Wife,* 2) *Cabaret,* 3) *Irma La Douce,* 4) *Milk and Honey,* 5) *South Pacific,* and 6) the 1968 production of *Hair* as well as all of its subsequent Broadway revivals.

352Q. Mrs. Bennet in *First Impressions* has five daughters, making for a family of six. Tevye has five daughters, making for a family of seven, which will expand to ten before *Fiddler* comes to an end.

And yet, there's one song in a musical that mentions even more members of a family if you include in-laws.

What's the song?

What's the musical?

353Q. She was already a world-famous character before she was musicalized in an off-Broadway show. Less remembered is that she had an Aunt Marion.

Who is she?

What's the musical?

What's the line that proves this?

354Q. In her first starring role in a musical (which was revived on Broadway both last century and this), she played a woman who's romantically linked with an Englishman with a title.

His character's surname is pronounced the same way as the character's surname that this performer would originate a dozen years later. The surnames are spelled differently, but they're pronounced the same.

Who's the performer?

What are the musicals?

What are the surnames and spellings of both characters?

355Q. What do these songs have in common?

1) "Finishing the Hat" (*Sunday in the Park with George*), 2) "Put on a Happy Face" (*Bye Bye Birdie*), 3) "Shy" (*Once Upon a Mattress*), and 4) "You Gotta Have Heart" (*Damn Yankees*).

356Q. Whose father in a world-famous musical called his daughter "Maruca"?

357Q. A Tony-nominated long-running musical set in the 1950s has a character who's seen only in act 2. Her first name is part of a song title that opens act 2 of a Tony-nominated long-running musical from the 1950s that's also set in the 1950s.

Who is she?

What's the name of the song?

What are the names of the musicals?

358Q. In 1959, two musicals that opened less than a month apart each had a song that included the name of the same Greta Garbo film.

The first to open ran more than a year and won a Tony for its leading man—the only Tony that the production won—but it's pretty much forgotten today. The second, however, ran more than three years and became world-famous.

Both mentions of the Garbo film were not sung by the musicals' leads but by supporting performers.

What's the name of the Garbo film?

What are the musicals in which it's mentioned?

What are the songs?

359Q. A Tony-winning musical opened with a bit of a song that had decades before been one of the Oscar nominees for Best Original Song in the first year that the award was given.

What's the song?

What's the musical?

360Q. This performer had a walk-on in a musical, for which she won a Tony. A walk-on!

Who is she?

What's the musical?

Explain that walk-on.

361Q. What do these musicals have in common:

1) Falsettos, 2) Flora the Red Menace, 3) *High Spirits,* and 4) *Honk!*

362Q. Less than a year after more than one songwriter was summoned to Detroit to add songs to his floundering musical—which became an enormous hit—this composer-lyricist was brought to Boston to add songs to someone else's floundering musical—a show that took place about a hundred years earlier.

He wound up putting two songs in the musical. Both of them started with the same two letters—in words that just happen to be homonyms, too.

Who is he?

What was his floundering musical?

What was the musical he helped?

What are the names of the two songs?

363Q. A Best Musical Tony and Pulitzer Prize–winning musical has two songs in a row in which an automobile is mentioned. The first of the two songs specifically cites a very high-end model; the second a far more plebian vehicle.

What's the musical?

What are the songs?

What are the automobiles?

364Q. What Tony-nominated composer-lyricist was married at the time to someone who'd eventually be mentioned in *The Full Monty?*

365Q. He appeared in a famous comic number in a very famous serious musical in the 1950s. The lyrics contained two words that would appear in an equally famous musical that he conceived in the 1970s.

Who's the person?

What's the 1950s song?

What's the 1950s musical

What's the two-word phrase in the 1970s musical?

Name that musical, too.

366Q. What did these five shows—all of which closed out of town—have in common?

1) *Annie 2: Miss Hannigan's Revenge,* 2) *The Baker's Wife,* 3) *Busker Alley,* 4) the 2003 revival of *The Miracle Worker,* and 5) *Paper Moon.*

367Q. She appeared in two Broadway musicals in the 1960s, received a nomination for each—and lost both times. She also recorded many songs from musicals from the early twentieth century to the late twentieth century.

One of them was "He Could Show Me" from *Now Is the Time for All Good Men,* a 1967 off-Broadway musical. Not only did she record the song, but she also paid for the show's cast album to be recorded.

Who is she?

368Q. There aren't that many show songs that have the letters *qu* in them. And yet, each and every one of a certain illustrious composer's musicals for which he provided a *complete* score saw one of his melodies either start with *qu* or include the letters *qu* in their titles.

Who's the composer?

What are the musicals?

What are the names of the songs?

369Q. Greta Garbo was a big silent film star, so when the talkies began, MGM advertised that in her next picture "Garbo Talks!"

A Broadway play in the 1960s used the same claim about a very different performer ("So-and-so talks!") in her second and final Broadway play. She'd already made a dynamic debut in her first one—one that later paid even bigger dividends in Hollywood when she won an Oscar for this famous role. (The Tony committee hadn't even given her a nomination.)

Who's the performer?

In what play did she barely talk?

In what play did she have a lot to say?

370Q. There's a Tony-winning musical from the 1950s that had a character actor win a Best Actor in a Musical Tony. At one point he describes another character as "a very attractive girl from Chicago." The statement turned out to be ironically accurate twenty years later.

Why?

371Q. What do these musicals have in common with Tony-winning musicals?

1) *Funny Face,* 2) *Legs Diamond,* 3) *Rent,* 4) *Ring of Fire,* and 5) *Tell Me More.*

372Q. A high-profile revival of a Shakespeare play not only was fully recorded on four records but also had a one-record highlights album. Most performers in its cast had at least one experience with a Broadway musical. It also had quite a few performers who would soon take to the musical stage.

What's the play?

Who are the performers?

In what musicals did they appear?

373Q. A person for whom a Broadway theater is now named was born on the street that's specifically mentioned in a famous song from a very successful mid-1940s movie musical.

It became a not-so-successful Broadway musical in the 1980s.
The stage version played a theater that was named for a much more
famous person.

(Hint: The two theaters are *not* named for performers.)

Who are the people for whom the theaters are named?

What's the name of the street that is mentioned in the song?

Name the song, too.

374Q. Take the first letter of the titles of these nine musicals, follow
each letter with a period, and what do you get?

1. It's still the most unlikely one-word title of any successful musical, let alone one that won the Best Book and Best Score Tonys.
2. Not just Roman Catholics, but many others love this musical
   that had many sequels.
3. The musical flop whose name was included in the title of a
   book about failed musicals.
4. A popular Irish film that became a popular Broadway musical.
5. A musical of a film that had more than two dozen songwriters
   receive a Tony nomination.
6. A musical about a lamentable chapter in Georgia history.
7. A vampire musical flop with music by a well-known
   composer-entertainer.
8. A British musical that became an international hit and a film
   that included a new song that won an Oscar.
9. A Tony-winning musical that had a five-word title when it
   opened but abridged it to one word during its Broadway run.

What's the word?

375Q. Only weeks before a new musical by Jerry Bock and Sheldon
Harnick was to go into rehearsal, the creators jettisoned their seven-
word title in favor of a much shorter one.

The last three words of that original discarded title became the
first three words of a popular off-Broadway revue of the 1990s. The

original Bock and Harnick title even had the same atypical punctuation as the revue, and was somewhat thematically linked to the revue's title.

What was the former name of the Bock and Harnick musical?

What was the new one?

What's the revue?

376Q. Why are these songs in this order?

1) "It's a Hell of a Way to Run a Love Affair" (*Plain and Fancy*), 2) "But, Mr. Adams" (*1776*), 3) "Why Am I Me?" (*Shenandoah*), 4) "Non Stop" (*Hamilton*), 5) "I Believe" (*The Book of Mormon*), 6) "Lights! Camera! Platitude!" (*What Makes Sammy Run?*), 7) "Satisfied" (*Hamilton*), and 8) "The Ballad of Czolgosz" (*Assassins*).

377Q. When talking about Best Musical Tony-winners, what do these losing nominees have in common?

1) Jay Blackton (*Redhead*), 2) Frank Loesser (*How to Succeed in Business Without Really Trying*, 3) Boris Aronson (*Fiddler on the Roof*), 4) William F. Brown (*The Wiz*), 5) Ken Billington, (*Sweeney Todd*), 6) Charles Nelson Reilly (*Hello, Dolly!*), and 7) Scott Pask (*The Band's Visit*).

378Q. If a song title from a Tony-winning musical of the 1970s had been written in time for June 13, 1965, it would have aptly described Chita Rivera's job situation that day.

Explain.

379Q. Why are these musicals in this order?

1) *The Drowsy Chaperone*, 2) *West Side Story*, 3) *The Most Happy Fella*, 4) *The Boys from Syracuse*, 5) *On Your Feet!*, 6) *Wicked*, 7) *Nine*, 8) *The Color Purple*, 9) *Mame*, 10) *Little Women*, 11) *Peter Pan*, 12) *The Producers*, 13) *Pacific Overtures*, 14) *Dude*, 15) *Grand Hotel*, 16) *Kiss Me, Kate*, 17) *The Hunchback of Notre Dame*, 18) *Grease*, 19) *Man of La Mancha*, 20) *Two Gentlemen of Verona*, 21) *Fioretta*, 22) *Sweet Charity*, 23) *On the Town*, 24) *City of Angels*, and 25) *Minnie's Boys*.

Note: There should be one more musical between *On the Town* and *City of Angels*. Give the reason why there isn't.

380Q. It's rare for a featured actor to be in a musical and never sing a note, but this actor did it twice—once in a 1950s stage musical that was a notorious flop, and once in a 1960s movie musical that was a smash hit—after it had been a smash stage hit, too.

However, you can at least hear him speak on the original cast album of a comic revue that has some incidental music.

Who is he?

What are all three properties?

381Q. He received a Tony nomination for appearing in what would become a Tony-winning musical. But on the current CD reissue of the original cast album, you'll only hear him do one song although he sang in five in the show.

Who is he?

What's the musical?

What's the explanation?

382Q. The end sequence of *1776* mentions all of the original thirteen colonies. But it's not a real song, is it? What actual song with a beginning, middle, and end—from the same decade in which *1776* was produced—indeed does mention all thirteen?

(Ironically, the musical's title includes the name of an international city.)

383Q. What do these shows have in common?

1) "Intermission Talk" (*Me and Juliet*), 2) "Nothing Can Replace a Man" (*Ankles Aweigh*), 3) "The Only Dance I Know" (*Mr. President*), 4) "Hello, 12, Hello 13, Hello Love" (*A Chorus Line*), 5) "Opening Doors" (*Merrily We Roll Along*), and 6) "My Psycho-Pharmacologist and I" (*next to normal*).

384Q. She was the star in the original cast of a famous and respected musical that has had more than one Broadway revival.

As acclaimed as she was in it—and she was—she never again appeared in a musical on Broadway. She did come close in what would become a notorious failure. But before that disaster opened on Broadway (and closed on the same night), her character had been eliminated.

Some years later, the actor who had portrayed the title character in this stage catastrophe would play the lead in the film version of her acclaimed hit stage musical.

Who is she?

Who is he?

What are the two musicals?

385Q. A song from an 1896 Broadway musical—yes, 1896!—had a few bars of it show up in a 1991 off-Broadway musical that came to Broadway thirteen years later.

What's the song?

What are the two musicals?

386Q. An early Lerner and Loewe flop has a character who, in a way, has something in common with a character in a late Rodgers and Hammerstein flop.

What is it?

387Q. What do these performers have in common?

1) P. J. Benjamin, 2) Ashley Brown, 3) Gloria De Haven, 4) Johnny Johnston, 5) Maria Karnilova, 6) Christopher Plummer, 7) Martin Short, 8) Laurence Naismith, and 9) Laurence Naismith. (There's a reason he's named twice.)

388Q. One of this famous writer's many, many plays was made into a film in the late 1930s. Another of his plays was made into a film in the early 1940s.

One of the first scenes in the latter film showed two actors who would share the stage in a 1950s smash hit world-famous musical; in fact, it was the musical version of the play that had become the 1930s film.

Moreover, the female star of that 1940s film was also the female star of the 1930s film that would inspire the 1950s smash hit musical.

What are the two plays?

Who are the two actors?

Who's the actress?

What's the musical?

389Q. When a certain controversial Tony-winning drama was adapted for network television, the first names of its four main characters—names already famous to the American public thanks to a *very* long-running television series—were changed to four others.

What's the play?

What were the characters' names in the stage production?

What were they in the television version?

Why were they changed?

390Q. A bookwriter-lyricist of a 1960s flop musical had in the previous decade written a Broadway hit comedy. Also involved in that success, albeit in a different capacity for him, was the leading man of an earlier 1960s flop musical that had been written by one of our greatest songwriting teams.

The bookwriter-lyricist and the actor had last names that *almost* rhyme. One surname has an *s* at the end. That man was best known for performing Shakespeare, but the nation came to know him in a popular sitcom some years later.

The bookwriter-lyricist also wrote a popular novel that when made into a film gave this same actor a small part.

Who are they?

What are the two musicals that they did independent of each other?

What's the comedy on which they worked together?

What's the film on which they worked together?

391Q. There haven't been many ties in Tony history, but one of them involved two musicals that had songs with almost identical titles.

One had a six-word title; the other had just five words in its title. Still, those five words were consecutively found in the first title.

What are the songs?

From what musicals did they come?

In what category was the tie?

Who were the cowinners?

392Q. If you check IBDB.com to see how many characters had the surname "Smith" in 1960s book musicals, you'll find listed Charlie Smith in *Subways Are for Sleeping* and Warren Smith in *On a Clear Day You Can See Forever.*

But there was another character who was born with the surname Smith that IBDB doesn't mention among those 1960s musicals. The actor who played him was the top-billed lead, too—and was cast in an earlier iteration of one of those above-mentioned musicals.

Who's this Smith?

In what musical did he appear?

Who played him?

And what early iteration of one of the listed musicals would he have done had the show not been scrapped?

393Q. What do these five songs have in common?

1) "Buddy's Blues" (*Follies*), 2) "He's a Genius" (*Darling of the Day*), 3) "No Lover" (*Out of This World*), 4) "I Am on My Way" (*Paint Your Wagon)*, and 5) "Six Months out of Every Year" (*Damn Yankees*).

394Q. You could hear him sing during the original production of *They're Playing Our Song*. Twenty-one years earlier, however, he had released an astonishingly popular "Greatest Hits" album that included a song from a flop musical of that decade.

Frankly, the song *wasn't* one of his greatest hits compared with many of his others on the record, but its songwriters were happy it was included, for the album stayed on the best-seller charts for most of the next ten years.

Who's the singer?

What did he sing in *They're Playing Our Song*?

What's the name of the song from the flop musical that he recorded?

From what musical does it come?

395Q. Most shows that close out of town are never heard from again. And yet, there was one play that greatly bucked those odds.

About a decade after its disastrous tryout, it resurfaced with a different title as a TV series that became wildly successful.

Just one more thing: Neil Simon saw one of his more serious plays headed by the star of this series.

Who's the star?

What's the series?

What's the Simon play in which he starred?

And just one more thing—what was the original name of the play that closed out of town?

396Q. In *Merrily We Roll Along,* on the opening night of the mythical show *Musical Husbands* its authors are in the lobby of the Alvin Theatre while their show is having its premiere. Composer Franklin Shepard's wife, Beth, is in her last days of pregnancy, prompting friend Mary Flynn to say, "Oh, Beth, please try not to have the baby right here or you might feel obligated to call it Alvin."

There's an inherent irony here. What is it?

397Q. An author wrote a novel that became a blockbuster film. Thirty-five years later, it became a Broadway play in which its leading lady was required to do a nude scene, albeit in very dim light.

The novelist's name is the same as the characters of the father and husband in one of the most famous plays to ever win a Pulitzer Prize.

What's the name of the novelist?

What's the name of the novel, film, and play (which are all the same)?

Who's the character with the same name?

In what Pulitzer Prize–winning play does he appear?

398Q. A husband and wife team once wrote a play about the difficulties they had with their teenage daughter. The performer playing the daughter won a Tony and has gone on to a decent career, but the actual daughter went on to an arguably better career, although not in the theater.

Who are the parents?

What's the name of their play?

Who was their daughter?

Who won a Tony for essentially playing her?

399Q. What do "Magic to Do" from *Pippin* and "Necessity" from *Finian's Rainbow* have in common?

400Q. When it closed after 957 performances in 1946, *Anna Lucasta* was not only the greatest success a play had ever had on Broadway with an African American cast but it had become one of Broadway's longest-running plays.

Now it's long forgotten, but in the 1950s it was still well enough remembered to be mentioned in a musical that starred a performer whose name now adorns a Broadway theater.

What's the musical?

What's the song?

Who's the star for which the theater was named?

401Q. Lyricists are encouraged not to use identities—where "rhymes" are made from different spellings but have the same sound.

An example can be found in *Hamilton* in "Dear Theodosia": "Oh, Philip, you outshine the morning sun" is followed by "My son." Different spellings, yes, but same exact sounds.

If you listen to *Bye Bye Birdie*'s original cast album, you'll find one.

What is it?

If you listen to its soundtrack, you'll find two.

What are they?

402Q. A mother had been appearing on Broadway for more than a quarter century when her daughter made her Broadway debut.

It was at a theater that her mother had never played in her ten Broadway appearances. Finally, for her eleventh musical, she would.

Who's the mother?

Who's the daughter?

What musicals did they do at this theater?

What's the name of the theater?

403Q. This major star who originated the leading role in a famous musical didn't receive a Tony nomination, let alone a Tony—albeit for a very specific reason.

But the equally esteemed major star who played that same role the following year *did* receive a Tony.

What's the musical?

Who originated the role?

Who succeeded the performer?

And for that matter, how could this possibly happen, given that replacements aren't usually eligible for Tonys?

404Q. Who was the first Oscar-winner to star in a musical directed by an Oscar-winner?

405Q. This performer appeared in a Rodgers and Hammerstein musical both on stage and on screen. Before those assignments, however, she recorded the 1953 hit song "Vaya Con Dios," Spanish for "Go with God."

Who's the performer?

What's the stage and screen musical?

406Q. From 1896 through the 1980s, consumers who made purchases at certain establishments were given S & H Green Stamps that they could eventually redeem for prizes.

So popular were they that two musicals in the 1960s had songs that mentioned such stamps. Although the two musicals from which these green-stamped songs came did not win Tonys as Best Musical, the composers and lyricists would eventually claim two Tony-winning Best Musicals to their credit.

What are the shows?

What are the songs?

Who were the composers and lyricists?

What were their Tony-winning musicals?

407Q. When this famous musical disaster premiered in the late 1980s at a now no-longer-used theater, its opening number included an Italian word.

Perhaps people didn't understand it, for in the early part of this new century, when this same number was used as the second song in a completely different musical, an English word was used instead—although that word didn't have the same meaning as the original one.

What's the song?

What are the words?

What are the two musicals?

408Q. If you listen to "Where Am I Going?" from *Sweet Charity*, you'll hear two words that had been chosen as the title of a play that was based on a famous novel of the same name and produced in the 1940s.

But the play version shuttered in Boston.

To everyone's surprise, before the year was out, the play came to Broadway and ran almost a year—but under a new title. With that second title, it's since had multiple Broadway revivals; the second one was the most successful, for it garnered four Tony Awards. A film version even won an Oscar for its leading lady.

What's the original title that was the same as the novel—the one that Charity mentions in a different context?

What's the second, more enduring title?

Who won the Oscar for the film version?

409Q. When writers turn novels into musicals, they sometimes retain the book's original title: *Show Boat, Tenderloin*, and *A Tree Grows in Brooklyn*.

Others, though, opt for a brand-new title: *The Adventures of Huckleberry Finn* (*Big River*); *Cry the Beloved Country* (*Lost in the Stars,*) and *My Love, My Love* (*Once on This Island*).

But the authors of one musical (including one who'd soon win a Pulitzer Prize) chose not to use the actual title of the classic. Instead, they chose the original author's earlier title for the book before she changed her mind and landed on the household-name title that much of the world has known for centuries.

What's the original name of the novel that is also the name of the musical?

What's the novel's well-known title?

410Q. In the history of awards, in what category did the musicals 1) *Miss Liberty,* 2) *Call Me Madam,* 3) *Wish You Were Here,* 4) *Damn Yankees,* 5) *Peter Pan,* 6) *The Music Man,* and 7) *Mr. President* all emerge victorious?

411Q. An actor and director worked on a musical for which the actor won a Tony; the director, however, wasn't even nominated.

The two had worked together before on a film about a famous theatrical family. But for that movie, the director of the musical wasn't the director but the screenwriter.

In the film, the actor got the chance to play a scene from the classic play—a play that he would do *in toto* as the next Broadway role he tackled after his Tony win.

Who's the actor?

Who's the director/screenwriter?

What's the musical?

What's the film?

What's the play?

412Q. No article mentions that Peter Allen and Robert Klein ever worked together on Broadway. But in a way—*in a way,* mind you—they did.

Explain.

413Q. As we established, Shirley Booth was the first performer in the twentieth century to have already won a competitive Oscar (for *Come Back, Little Sheba*) and then was heard on an original cast album (*By the Beautiful Sea*).

But who was the first person to have won a competitive Oscar in the *twentieth* century and was then heard on a *twenty-first-century* original cast album?

414Q. *The Pajama Game* was the first Broadway musical to use a Dictaphone within a song. Someone very much involved with that show was connected—albeit in a different capacity—to the first Broadway musical to use an answering machine within a song.

Who is he?

What's the musical?

What's the song?

415Q. What musical revue makes reference to 1) *Aida,* 2) *Gentlemen Prefer Blondes,* 3) *Guys and Dolls,* 4) *The King and I,* 5) *Call Me Madam,* and 6) *South Pacific?*

416Q. Two writers who always worked together wrote eight Broadway plays and four Broadway musicals—one of which ran over fifteen hundred performances.

One of their plays, however, couldn't reach fifteen performances. It was a fictional take on a person who became the subject of a world-famous musical that also ran over fifteen hundred performances.

Who were the writers?

What was their long-running hit musical?

What was their shortest-running play?

Who was the subject of the musicals and the unsuccessful play?

417Q. Someone who's been represented on Broadway most of the years of the last half of the twentieth century had a father whose first name appears in one title of a hit Broadway production.

The production won a Tony for its leading man, but that actor who won it wasn't in the play. We'll reiterate, for it does sound impossible, doesn't it? The show won a Tony for its leading man, but that actor who won wasn't in the play.

There *is* a way that such a situation could happen—and did.

Explain.

418Q. Ruth Sherwood would be able to get this one.

What do these musicals have in common?

1) *One Touch of Venus,* 2) *Cry for Us All,* 3) *The Look of Love,* 4) *A Night with Janis Joplin,* and 5) *Rocky.*

419Q. As of this writing, twelve currently active Broadway theaters have never had the pleasure or honor of having a Tony-winning musical originate in their houses.

What are they?

420Q. What was the last Broadway musical to be filmed in black and white?

421Q. He was a vaudevillian who appeared in four musicals nearly a hundred years ago: *Hassard Short's Ritz Revue, Gay Paree, Piggy,* and *Cross My Heart.*

His wife's name will remind you of a character in a Tony-winning 1960s musical that became a high-grossing film as well as a TV movie.

What is his name?

What is her name?

422Q. One hit 1960s musical had a producer, a director-choreographer, a bookwriter-lyricist, a composer, and *an entire cast* who had either previously worked on—or would eventually work on—a musical (or musicals) that closed out of town and avoided a Broadway humiliation.

What was the hit musical on which they all worked?

Give the names and out-of-town closings that each person either had or would experience.

423Q. What do these songs have in common?

1) "All I Care about Is Love" (*Chicago*), 2) "Arthur in the Afternoon" (*The Act*), 3) "Don't Forget 127th Street" (*Golden Boy*), 4) "The Harvard Variations" (*Legally Blonde*), 5) "Little Tin Box" (*Fiorello!*), 6) "A Lot of Livin' to Do" (*Bye Bye Birdie*), 7) "Repent" (*On the Twentieth Century*), 8) "The Rich" (*The Cradle Will Rock*), 9) "Takin' It Slow" (*Pump Boys and Dinettes*).

424Q. *The Subject Was Roses,* which eventually won a Best Play Tony and Pulitzer Prize, opened so late in the 1963–1964 season that it didn't make *The Best Plays* book of that year, but was carried over to the next year. That had never happened with any other play or musical.

What also had never happened with any other play or musical is that it ran 832 performances.

And yet, *The Subject Was Roses* also has one more distinction that no other Broadway play or musical has ever, ever had.

What is it?

425Q. For a while during its genesis, *Pippin* almost had a title that had something in common with a Tony-nominated Best Musical that was the last to open in a previous decade.

What's the commonality?

What's the other musical?

426Q. Two actresses each won a Tony on the same night—one for a musical, one for a play.

Each ended her show's first act with a song—the same song, which is one of the most famous musical theater songs from a musical that has seen many revivals.

What's the song?

Who are the two Tony-winners who sang it?

In what show did each sing it?

427Q. From 1906 through 1987, a name could be found in the cast list in *Playbill* in every one of those nine decades.

It could be found as few as twice in the 1960s but as many as thirty-seven times in the 1920s.

What's the name?

428Q. In *Carousel,* after Julie Jordan had married Billy Bigelow, if she'd decided to use the initials of her first name and maiden name, she'd be J. J. Bigelow.

Name another character in a Rodgers and Hammerstein musical who, if she'd decided to do the same thing, would then have the same name of a British novelist who used his two initials before his last name.

(One of his novels was adapted into an early 1960s Broadway play that retained the novel's name.)

429Q. A dozen actors made a film that was turned into a Broadway play many moons later.

Each of them was in the original cast of the following Broadway shows—some before the film, some after. These properties are listed in this order for a certain reason:

1) *Nowhere To Go But Up,* 2) *A Raisin in the Sun,* 3) *Death of a Salesman,* 4) *Waiting for Godot,* 5) *Gypsy,* 6) *Caligula,* 7) *The Body Beautiful,* 8) *Mr. Roberts,* 9) *The Crucible,* 10) *All My Sons,* 11) *The Physicists,* and 12) *Period of Adjustment.*

430Q. This actor first appeared in a musical whose male star had a famous solo in a Rodgers and Hammerstein musical.

His second appearance was in a musical that lasted one week and starred an actor whose wife's fame had far eclipsed his by this time.

His third and final musical had already won a Best Musical Tony when he joined it as a replacement; it would run thousands of performances.

All this happened in the 1960s—the same decade in which a film was released that had a prominent character with the same name as this actor. In the next century, that film was made into a Tony-winning musical that lasted even longer than the one just cited.

Identify all the actors and musicals.

What's the name of the character?

431Q. If you looked at the window card or the original Broadway cast album of this two-month flop—not the off-Broadway revival cast album, mind you, but the original Broadway cast album —you just might assume from the logo that the show had a six-word title and not a four-word title.

(Hint: The artist who drew the logo became a Tony-winning playwright.)

What's the musical?

What's the explanation?

432Q. What musical had the longest Broadway run without recording an original cast album?

433Q. An off-Broadway original cast album with a score by a future two-time Tony-winning songwriter has a song that mentions these Broadway attractions: 1) *The Andersonville Trial,* 2) *The Gang's All Here,* 3) *The Miracle Worker,* 4) *J. B.,* 5) *Juno,* 6) *Our Town,* 7) *Rashomon,* 8) *Sweet Bird of Youth,* 9) *The Tenth Man,* 10) *The World of Suzie Wong,* and 11) *Fiorello!*

What is the song?

From what revue does it come?

434Q. What do these musical adaptations all have in common?

1) *Anastasia,* 2) *Seventeen,* 3) *Some Like It Hot,* 4) *Let It Ride!,* and 5) *Oh, Brother!*

435Q. In the 1980s, the bookwriter, composer, and lyricist—each of whom had already won two Tonys—worked on a musical that had a song with this lyric:

"The wait for critics is a bitch but here's a very lucky switch: We win approval from Frank Rich (even though it isn't Sondheim)."

By the time the show opened, the song was dropped because the new bookwriter—also a two-time Tony-winner—succeeding the original one (who had died) suggested moving the action to many years earlier.

What's the musical?

Who are the three writers?

Why was the song dropped?

436Q. What musical from the 1990s that played on West 46th Street has homonyms in the last name of its composer and the first name of its lyricist?

(Hint: Both of them had won Tonys in the 1960s.)

437Q. In the early 1960s, each was the star of a musical flop that couldn't even reach a hundred performances.

In the 1950s, however, they were in a more successful musical for which each won a Tony. They also shared the same birthday—although he was substantially older than she.

Who were they?

What were the names of their quick flops?

For what musical did they win their Tonys?

What is the date of their birthdays?

438Q. Why are these Sondheim songs listed in this order?

1) "Simple," 2) "Happily Ever After," 3) "Everybody Ought to Have a Maid," 4) "I Know Things Now," 5) "Later," and 6) "Another National Anthem."

439Q. The 1948 film *The Snake Pit* dealt with a woman who, because of a trauma or two, became mentally unbalanced every time May 12 rolled around.

What notorious musical with a different mentally unbalanced character opened on May 12 (but didn't stay open for long)?

440Q. The original cast of each of these plays had one performer that was mentioned in the opening song of a 1970s musical.

The order in which they're mentioned in song are 1) *Mary, Mary;* 2) *Darkness at Noon;* 3) *Mr. Big;* 4) *Everywhere I Roam;* and 5) *The Late George Apley.*

Who are the performers?

What's the opening song?

What is the musical?

441Q. During the 1970s, one revival of a comedy and one revival of a musical both closed on the same night. The comedy played in the conventional theater district; the musical was housed about a dozen blocks north.

The musical was a revival of a British import that had originally arrived here in the 1960s; it had a song in it that was the actual name of the comedy.

What was the name of the revived comedy that was also the name of the song?

From what musical does it come?

442Q. What do these musicals have in common?

1) *The Happy Time,* 2) the 1976 revival of *My Fair Lady,* 3) the 1981 revival of *The Pirates of Penzance,* 4) *City of Angels,* 5) *Ragtime,* 6) *Dirty Rotten Scoundrels,* and 7) *Kinky Boots.*

443Q. He turned down the offer to play the lead in a 1960s musical. The actor who took the role won a Tony in this Tony-winning musical.

That Tony-winner repeated the role in the film version, with the actor who'd turned down the lead appearing in a featured role.

However, a few years later, that other actor finally came to Broadway and played the leading role for which he was originally sought— and won a Tony for it, too.

Who is he?

What's the musical?

What's the role he turned down but eventually played?

What's the role he had in the film version?

444Q. For thirty-two of the first sixty-six months of the 1970s, the sound of the Andrews Sisters could be heard on Broadway.

Explain.

445Q. The name of a famous character who has been lionized in comic books, a TV series, and films has been seen twice on the marquee of the same Broadway theater.

It first happened with a revival of a play by an esteemed playwright, and then happened again many years later in a new musical.

Granted, the playwright didn't have the comic book character in mind, but he did just happen to cite someone who'd been on the cultural scene for a few years.

Who's the comic book character?

What's the play that was revived?

What's the musical?

What's the theater?

446Q. What commonality will you discover if you listen to the original cast album and hear these songs?

1) "A Fact Can Be a Beautiful Thing" (*Promises, Promises*), 2) "Little Jazz Bird" (*My One and Only*), 3) "My Way" (*The Roar of the Greasepaint—The Smell of the Crowd*), 4) "Scream" (*I Love My Wife*), and 5) "Wild West Show/Dog Act" (*The Will Rogers Follies*).

447Q. When Faye Dunaway agreed to partake in the 1964 Repertory Theatre of Lincoln Center revival of *The Changeling*, she was in fact agreeing with one of Dimitri Weismann's Girls.

Explain.

448Q. Why are these musicals listed in this order?

1) *The Prom*, 2) *Evita*, 3) *Into the Woods*, 4) *Hair*, 5) *Gypsy*, 6) *Peter Pan*, and 7) *The Chocolate Soldier*.

449Q. What musical nominated for seven Tonys (but won none) mentions a total of eight presidents in three of its songs: the first, third, seventh, sixteenth, thirtieth, thirty-first, thirty-third, and thirty-fourth?

(Considering when the musical played, the lyricist went about as far as he could go.)

450Q. Maureen Stapleton, Robert Morse, Robert Preston, and Helen Gallagher are among the comparatively few performers to win two Tony Awards.

But what is distinctive about the ones they won?

451Q. What do these musicals have in common?

1) *New Faces of 1952,* 2) *Whoop-Up,* 3) *On a Clear Day You Can See Forever,* 4) *The Book of Mormon,* and 5) *Groundhog Day.*

452Q. Not many characters in musicals are named Vernon, but you'd find one in two consecutive Tony-winning musicals.

What were the shows?

453Q. A smash hit musical that has name recognition even with people who know virtually nothing about musicals opened forty-seven years to the day after a comedy whose title was a parody of the musical's source material.

What's the name of the musical?

What was the name of the far, far less successful comedy?

454Q. A little less than twenty years before this major musical hit officially opened, its composer's father was the sole musician in a very short-lived Broadway play.

It played in the theater directly behind the theater where his son's major hit would play its entire, record-breaking run.

What are the names of both people?

To what shows were they connected?

What are the theaters?

455Q. What's odd about the shows that opened on Broadway on January 17, 2008; August 16, 1917; and September 16, 1935; respectively?

456Q. What do these plays have in common?

1) *Angel Street,* 2) *God of Carnage,* 3) *Indians,* 4) *Sexual Perversity in Chicago,* and 5) *The Time of the Cuckoo.*

457Q. A song in a mid-1960s musical that opened in May had a song title that mentioned two occupations. One of the jobs would be mentioned in a musical that would open that September, while the other job would be mentioned in a musical that would open in October.

The September musical was a smash hit; the October one was a near miss. As for the musical from which the song comes, it was doing capacity business until the star left in a controversy.

What's the song?

From what musical did it come?

What occupation is named in the September musical?

What occupation is named in the October musical?

458Q. They functioned as backup singers to the star in a 2010 musical. Some years later, one of them landed a part in a high-profile revival before deciding not to do it. Her replacement was the other former backup singer who eventually had to be very glad things turned out the way they did.

What are the musicals involved?

Who are the performers?

What's the reason that one of them wound up happy?

459Q. The 1949 film musical *Take Me out to the Ball Game* deals with players who must learn how to collaborate with a female owner.

What leading lady who did one and only one Broadway musical (by Rodgers and Hammerstein) was part owner of a major-league baseball team that was located in her hometown?

(If you know the name of her memoir, you'll know the name of the city.)

460Q. What do the following have in common?

1) Sally Durant Plummer (*Follies*), 2) Lorelei Lee (*Gentlemen Prefer Blondes; Lorelei*), 3) Leo and Lucille Frank (*Parade*), 4) Lieutenant

Frank Cioffi (*Curtains*), and 5) Alvin, Cleo, Harvey, Monica, Norman, Quentin, Stanley, and Wally (*I Love My Wife*).

461Q. Two people who died in 1947—both of whom were highly political and involved in military service—eventually became characters in two Tony-winning musicals. One opened a week before the other.

Who are they?

In what musicals do they appear?

462Q. An actress starred in the first film versions of two Tony-nominated and much-revived Broadway musicals.

In the first film, she had a lyric that involved a mirror. In the second film, which followed a year later, she actually looked into a mirror and then said a line of dialogue that was very similar to the lyric.

Who is she?

What were the films?

What was the lyric and the song in the first film?

Describe the moment in the second.

463Q. Some musicals amass many more performances than the plays on which they were based. The musical version of *Chicago,* thanks to its 1996 revival, has reached five figures; the original play clocked 172, little more than a tenth of the musical revival's run.

However, what play ran on Broadway the shortest number of performances that later became a musical that had an even shorter run?

464Q. A twenty-first-century musical that had a return engagement two years after its Broadway premiere has a song that is twenty-six letters long. It also paraphrases a famous quotation from *Hamlet*.

What's the song?

From what musical does it come?

465Q. A film of a famous play by a legendary playwright—one that was later remade as a 1996 TV movie—starts with a shot of the Palace Theatre where the musical *Goodtime Charley* is playing.

The musical could only amass 104 performances, so that short run should help you to know what the acclaimed film was. But if you need a hint, someone involved with it won an Oscar.

What's the film?

Who won the Oscar?

466Q. "It's Not Where You Start, It's Where You Finish" was not originally written for *Seesaw*; composer Cy Coleman and lyricist Dorothy Fields created it for a musical that never was produced.

However, that musical had the same title and dealt with the same subject as a mythical musical that was mentioned repeatedly in the first scene of a twenty-first-century musical.

What musical is that?

Who was its subject?

467Q. A certain type of song is called "the want song," in which a character tells what he or she most desires. Sometimes that's done obliquely: "My Shot," *Hamilton*; "Not for the Life of Me," *Thoroughly Modern Millie*; "You and Me (But Mostly Me)," *The Book of Mormon*.

But some musicals come down to brass tacks by using the word "want" in their want songs. The musicals cited below did.

Name the want songs.

1) *Funny Girl,* 2) *Dreamgirls,* 3) *Baby,* 4) *Grand Hotel,* 5) *Bullets over Broadway,* and 6) *Ain't Too Proud.*

468Q. The day on which it received ten Tony nominations, including the one for Best Musical, was the eleventh anniversary of the opening of a play that had the same title.

What's the name of the musical and the play?

469Q. This character was already a household name in another medium when two bookwriters decided (strangely enough) to use her name for a supporting character in their new musical.

Nearly eighteen years later, two different librettists used her name again, which was understandable, for they were specifically writing for the character who originally made the name famous.

The first Broadway iteration of the character did not get a Tony nomination for its actress, because Best Featured Actress in a Musical was not yet a category.

By the time the second iteration came about, the Best Featured Actress in a Musical category had been long established, and now the performer who had played the character received a nomination.

What is the name of the characters?

In what musicals did they respectively appear?

Who played them?

Who received the nomination?

470Q. Eliza Doolittle longed for the day when she would "go to St. James so often I will call it St. Jim."

What twenty-first-century musical did go to the St. James, and if "St. Jim" doesn't come immediately to mind, a term very much like it should.

What's the musical?

What is the term?

471Q. What do these songs have in common?

1) "It's Today" (*Mame*), 2) "Poor Everybody Else" (*Seesaw*), 3) "Say a Prayer for Me Tonight" (*Gigi*), 4) "Something Was Missing" (*Annie*), and 5) "You'll Never Get Away from Me" (*Gypsy*).

472Q. Two musicals whose every word was written by the same bookwriter-lyricist were the shortest-running musicals to have two Tony-winners billed above their titles.

Who's the bookwriter-lyricist?

Who are the performers with star billing?

What were the musicals?

473Q. What do these plays have in common?

1) *The Little Foxes,* 2), *A Streetcar Named Desire,* 3) *Our Town,* 4) *Othello,* and 5) *A Midsummer Night's Dream.*

474Q. In *Ben Franklin in Paris,* Robert Preston actually mentions the next musical he would do on Broadway.

How?

475Q. What twenty-first-century film version of a 1980s musical uses a few measures of a song from a 1970s musical as background music?

(Hint: Both musicals had music and lyrics by the same person.)

476Q. What do these shows have in common?

1) *Brigadoon;* 2) *Mary, Mary;* 3) *Oh, Dad, Poor Dad, Mamma's Hung You in the Closet and I'm Feelin' So Sad;* 4) *Kiss Me, Kate;* 5) *No Strings;* 6) *Mummenschanz;* and 7) *Never Too Late.*

477Q. When she wrote the lyrics for one of the first musicals produced in a new decade, she used her first and last name.

When she wrote the lyrics for one of the last musicals produced in that same decade, she added a married name—although by that point she'd been divorced from that husband and was dating the show's composer.

Who is she?

For what musicals did she provide lyrics?

Who was the composer she was dating at the time of the second musical?

478Q. The Oscar-winning "Baby It's Cold Outside" comes from a film whose name is mentioned in a 1980s Broadway musical flop whose composer had enjoyed a major 1960s hit.

What's the name of the film?

What are the musical and the song that mentions it?

Who's the composer?

479Q. What producing artistic director of a theater company that centers on new musicals and vintage ones has the same name as a character in a Charles Strouse and Lee Adams musical flop?

480Q. What do these songs have in common?

1) "A Sleeping Bee" (*House of Flowers*), 2) "Some People" (*Gypsy*), 3) "Forever and a Day" (*High Spirits*), and 4) "Springtime for Hitler" (*The Producers*).

481Q. A character in a late Richard Rodgers musical has a boyfriend named Alfredo.

What's the musical?

What's the name of the character?

482Q. What characters in a Best Musical Tony-winner were engaged after having known each other little more than a month. Despite the whirlwind courtship, they have celebrated at least seventeen anniversaries.

Who are they?

What's the musical?

483Q. Why did *The Zulu and the Zayda*, scheduled to open on November 9, 1965, not open until November 10, 1965?

(Hint: The answer could be found in *Fly by Night*, a 2014 off-Broadway musical.)

484Q. His first assignment in a Broadway musical was taking over for a star who had won a Tony for the role. He followed that by replacing a star who'd won a Tony in his previous Broadway assignment.

Then he played a featured role in a famous film with a few songs in it. In the twenty-first century, it became a Broadway musical. Both his role and his song were omitted from the stage musical.

Who is he?

In what musicals did he replace stars?

What Tony-winners did he replace?

What's the film in which he appeared?

What was the name of his character and the song that didn't make the stage musical?

485Q. What do these numbers from the 1966–1967 Tony-nominated musicals have in common?

1) "Willkommen" (*Cabaret*), 2) "Nobody's Perfect" (*I Do! I Do!*), 3) "Walking Happy" (*Walking Happy*), and 4) "Oh, to Be a Movie Star" and 5) "Gorgeous" (*The Apple Tree*).

486Q. A 2006 Best Musical Tony-nominee had a song that mentioned a song from a Best Musical Tony-nominee that had been produced forty seasons earlier.

What are the songs?

From what musicals do they come?

487Q. Many major Broadway songwriters of the twentieth century wrote musicals that were set in France.

Which one had the highest percentage of book musicals to which he had provided songs?

488Q. It's a world-famous novella, but it hasn't had any luck with musical adaptations. A team that wrote what was once the longest-running musical in Broadway history provided the score for a film adaption, which didn't do well.

A few years later, a team that had won a Best Song Oscar collaborated with a three-time Tony-winning bookwriter—and their version shuttered in previews.

A third attempt was made in the twenty-first century; it was more of a dance piece than a musical, and couldn't last a month.

What is the apparently unadaptable novella?

Who wrote the three attempts?

489Q. What do these songs have in common?

1) "Terrace at Pau" (*Aspects of Love*), 2) The reprise of "Send in the Clowns" (*A Little Night Music*), 3) "Intermission Talk" (*Me and Juliet*), 4) "It's Not about Me" (*The Prom*), 5) "I Fought Every Step of the Way" (*Top Banana*), and 6) "Love Has Driven Me Sane" (*Two Gentlemen of Verona*).

490Q. We were all impressed when Stephen Sondheim wrote "Today I woke too weak to walk" in "Love, I Hear" in *A Funny Thing Happened on the Way to the Forum*. He used "woke," "weak," "walk"— three words that had the same sound at the beginning and end, but a different vowel sound in between. Brilliant!

But there's a musical that opened less than three years later whose lyricist made an even more deft move with the word "fraud." He found five words that have the same sound at the beginning and end with a different vowel sound in between.

What's the musical?

What's the song?

491Q. A play from the 1930s was made into a film in the 1940s. It was then remade as a musical movie in the 1950s under a new title— for a very good reason.

In the 1990s, it came to Broadway under its second title, for it couldn't have used the play's original title for the same good reason.

What's the name of the play?

What's the name of the musical movie and the stage musical?

Why did the title need to be changed?

492Q. *The Unemployed Saint, The Stars Weep,* and *Let Me Hear the Melody* all closed before they could reach Broadway. Yet one cast member in each would later work together in a musical that was this now-legendary composer's Broadway debut.

Who were the cast members?

Who was the future legendary composer?

What was the musical?

493Q. Although many of the questions in this book have asked "What do these musicals have in common?," these Tony-winning musicals actually have *two* commonalities. What are they?

1) *Redhead,* 2) *Two Gentlemen of Verona,* 3) *Passion,* 4) *Thoroughly Modern Millie,* and 5) *Billy Elliot.*

494Q. *Here's Where I Belong* ran for just one performance on Broadway, closing after opening night. *Hurry, Harry* managed to run two, and *Soon* racked up three.

Despite their lack of success, these twentieth-century musicals were all remembered in a song in a twenty-first-century musical.

What's the song?

From what musical does it come?

495Q. A multiple Tony-winning composer of two Best Musical Tony-winners in this century has the same surname as the actual surname of a female character—the *actual* surname, mind you—who appeared in an enormous failure that was written by a composer who had had three Tony-winning musicals.

Who's the composer of the three Tony-winning musicals who provided the music for the enormous failure?

Who's the two-time Tony-winning composer who has the same surname of the character?

In what show does she appear?

Before we close this section, let's have some mashups in which the names of two musicals are joined together. For example:

The Music Man of La Mancha

Flying over Sunset Boulevard

Flower Drum Song of Norway

Song & Dance a Little Closer

None of those mashups involve musicals in which the first show has any particular affinity with the second. *But:*

496Q. There's a very famous musical that won six Tonys (including Best Musical) that would come first in a mashup with an acclaimed musical with a legendary star that predated the Tony era.

Both were directed by the same man, although the earlier one had a book by him, too.

What's the mashup?

Who's the man in question?

497Q. There could be a mashup of two musicals with scores by one of Broadway's most famous songwriting teams.

The composer and lyricist won a Best Score Tony for a Tony-winning musical a dozen years after winning a Best Score Tony for a Tony-nominated musical.

What's the mashup?

Who are the composer and lyricist?

498Q. These two legends share the same birthday, although one was born eighteen years before the other.

The older of the two had a big Broadway flop that could be mashed up with the younger one's biggest flop that closed out of town.

What's the mashup?

Who are the two legends?

499Q. Do the math:

1. Start with the amount of money that the kids fantasize about in *The Me Nobody Knows*. (Make certain that you include the dollar sign, for the answer to this question will involve money.)

2. Divide it by the number of dollars that Mrs. Primrose is allegedly giving to Oscar Jaffee in *On the Twentieth Century*.

3. Subtract in dollars the number of warships that the Fisherman sees in *Pacific Overtures*.

4. Divide by the number of "nobodies in New York" mentioned in *[title of show]*.

5. Divide by the number of ladies with whom the Emcee cavorts in *Cabaret*.

6. Subtract in cents the number of duel commandments mentioned in *Hamilton*.

7. Divide by the number of spouses that the Baker in *Into the Woods* learns will be necessary to get the four items that he and his wife need.

What do you have?

Finally

For those who have been much too overtaxed by all of these brainteasers and would like to say to the author "You could drive a person crazy!" come! I'll make it easier for you with one last question:

500Q. In what year does the musical *1776* take place?

PHOTOFEST

Question: These men are dancing because they believe soon they'll be rich, but the joy they're feeling will soon be scuttled. The actors playing them won't be so happy, either; they'll only get four months' work from this musical, and none will get as much as a Tony nomination. However, the actress who played the character that sent them to their doom not only received the show's only acting nomination, but also won a Best Actress in a Musical Tony (for the second time). Who was she? What's the musical?

Answer: In the 1969 musical *Dear World*, these speculators will be sent into Parisian sewers by Countess Aurelia, played by Tony-winner Angela Lansbury.

PHOTOFEST

Question: One of the title characters as well as the locale of this "musical" take their names from members of the Phylum Chordata and the Class Actinopterygii. Who is the character? What's the locale? What's the name of the show that is set there?

Answer: Both a porgy and a catfish belong to Chordata and Actinopterygii. Catfish Row is the setting for the opera *Porgy and Bess*.

PHOTOFEST

Question: They appeared together in a landmark musical of the 1940s, but in the 1950s, on separate occasions, they filled in for the stars of a show written by the same gentlemen who'd provided them with their first smash hit. Who's he? Who's she? What's the musical they did together? Whom did they spell in what musical?

Answer: Alfred Drake and Celeste Holm were the original Curly and Ado Annie in Rodgers and Hammerstein's *Oklahoma!* In 1952, during the run of R&H's *The King and I*, Holm filled in for Gertrude Lawrence during her vacation; in 1953, Drake spelled Yul Brynner during his.

PHOTOFEST

Question: No, these teens in the 1960s hadn't tired of dancing the Monkey and the Pony and thus embraced the Caterpillar; this was a maneuver to win a football game. It was the brainchild of a character portrayed by an actor who was most famous for playing someone who didn't have a brain at all. (Look closely, and you'll see him in the picture.) What's the musical? Who's the actor playing the character who thought of this football play?

Answer: Ray Bolger, best known as the brainless scarecrow in *The Wizard of Oz*, portrayed Professor Fodorski in the 1962 musical *All American*. In it, he applied his expertise in engineering to football, ensuring that Southern Baptist Institute of Technology would have a winning season.

PHOTO BY MARTHA SWOPE ©BILLY ROSE THEATRE DIVISION,
THE NEW YORK PUBLIC LIBRARY FOR THE PERFORMING ARTS

Question: The gentleman on the far right is best known from his roles in film versions of Broadway musicals. Still, he did appear on Broadway in musicals by Rodgers, Hammerstein, Arlen, Mercer—as well as Don Gohman and Hal Hackady. Those last two were responsible for the musical pictured here. Who is he? What's this musical?

Answer: Before Howard Keel starred in the film versions of *Annie Get Your Gun*; *Show Boat*; *Kiss Me, Kate*; *Rose Marie*; and *Kismet*, he replaced the leads in the original Broadway productions of *Oklahoma!* and *Carousel*. After making those Hollywood films, he returned to Broadway in *Saratoga*, replaced Richard Kiley in *No Strings*, and made his final appearance in *Ambassador*, a nine-performance flop, pictured here.

PHOTOFEST

Question: There's no question that our eyes are drawn to the actress in the gold lame dress. Nevertheless, look among the men and see if you can find an actor who became a household name through a long-running TV series that had the greatest number of viewers watching its final episode. Who is he? What's the musical?

Answer: Alan Alda, later the star of the iconic TV series *M*A*S*H* (whose finale was watched by 105 million viewers), can be seen at the far left in the number "You Are Not Real" from the 1966 musical *The Apple Tree*.

PHOTOFEST

Question: Although Cyril Ritchard is smiling in this photograph, you needn't infer that he's the title character of the musical pictured here. What is the name of the show?

Answer: Despite Mr. Ritchard's efforts to look feminine, he was not the title character of *The Happiest Girl in the World*.

PHOTOFEST

Question: The gentleman whose head is in the lovely lady's lap played the eldest son in a long-running TV series set in the wild west. In it, he sported a hefty head of hair that was actually a toupée. Not until he appeared in this short-running musical did he reveal that he was bald. Who is he? What's the musical?

Answer: He's Pernell Roberts, certainly more famous as Adam Cartwright in TV's *Bonanza* than Captain Henry LaFarge in *Mata Hari*, which closed in Washington.

PHOTOFEST

Question: Extra! Extra! Hey, look at the two headlines! Historical news is being made! However, considering what happened on opening night of the musical that used this prop, write what might have been the first and second headlines of the next day's *Le Figaro*.

Answer: "Mata Hari Didn't Die! Scratched Nose after Shot 'Dead.'" For indeed, that is what actress Marisa Mell did after she'd been "fatally" hit by a firing squad's barrage of bullets.

PHOTOFEST

Question: No, that's not Helen Hayes being lifted up high by two strong men. However, this actress was known as "The Jewish Helen Hayes." Who is she? What is this musical in which she appeared?

Answer: She's Molly Picon, who played a widow looking for a husband while in Israel in Jerry Herman's first musical: *Milk and Honey*.

PHOTOFEST

Question: For a record 435 episodes, this real-life family appeared on America's TV screens. (And yet, try to find anyone who can remember the plot of a single show.) They became so iconic that a playwright used their actual names for his very different characters in his searing drama that would win a Tony. Who were they? What was the name of their TV show? What was the play that used their names?

Answer: Ozzie, Harriet, David, and Ricky Nelson starred in *The Adventures of Ozzie and Harriet*, a most aggrandizing title considering that what happened on each episode was hardly an "adventure." Because they seemed to be the quintessential prototype of the well-adjusted, happy-go-lucky family, playwright David Rabe chose their first names for his 1972 Tony-winning play *Sticks and Bones* that showed a very different American family at odds about the Vietnam War.

PHOTOFEST

Question: This musical was based on a novel that won a National Book Award and a film that won a Best Picture Oscar. Alas, the fate of this musical was not to be as sunny. What is it?

Answer: Richard Llewellyn's 1939 novel *How Green Was My Valley* won the 1940 National Book Award. Its film version even bested *Citizen Kane* in the 1941 Best Picture Oscar race. However, in 1966, its musical version called *A Time for Singing*, could only muster forty-one performances.

PART ONE

ANSWERS

IT'S THE HARD-KNOCK LIFE

1A. All of them have a song that begins with the word "Welcome."

1) to the Theater, 2) to the Rock, 3) to Falsettoland, 4) to the '60s, 5) to Hollywood, 6) to Holiday Inn, 7) My Party, 8) to the Night, and 9) to the Renaissance.

(It's our way of welcoming you to *Brainteasers for Broadway Geniuses*.)

2A. LuPone was the title character in the 1976 Stephen Schwartz–Joseph Stein musical *The Baker's Wife* that closed in Washington.

Joanna Gleason enjoyed Tony-winning success as the Baker's Wife in the original production of *Into the Woods*.

3A. All have reprises late in the musical.

1) "Proud of Your Boy," 2) "You Will Be Found," 3) "Way Down Hadestown," 4), "The Story of Tonight," 5) "Price and Son Theme," 6) "I'm Not That Girl," 7) "Stupid with You," 8) "Ireland," and 9) "There's a Fine, Fine Line."

4A. "Twelve Days to Christmas" from *She Loves Me* starts on the 13th, and then respectively announces nine days, four days, and one day before the 25th of December arrives.

5A. Nathan Lane, who won a Tony for *The Producers*, sang "Where Did We Go Right?" with Matthew Broderick.

Some years later in *The Addams Family*, for which he wasn't nominated, he sang "Where Did We Go Wrong?" with Bebe Neuwirth.

6A. All have songs that state "I love you" in the title.

1) "I've Never Said I Love You," 2) "Broadway, I Love You," 3) "Baby, I Love You," 4) "Do I Love You Because You're Beautiful?" 5) "The 'I Love You' Song," 6) "I Love You Like a Table," and 7) "As I Love You."

7A. *Annie 2,* which didn't even make it to Broadway but shuttered in Washington, was officially known as *Annie 2: Miss Hannigan's Revenge.*

Drop the last two words, and you'll get *Annie 2: Miss* (which indeed it was).

8A. Each production had a winner whose surname began with "Mc."

1) Ian McKellen, 2) Donna McKechnie, 3) Frances McDormand, 4) Michael McGrath, 5) Audra McDonald, and 6) Myron McCormick.

9A. In the song "Endgame," there's the lyric "The late Mr. 'S' has better chances of winning the Kentucky Derby than keeping his title today."

10A. In *Sweeney Todd,* Johanna enters the bakehouse, and while she's upset at seeing the dead bodies of Lucy and Sweeney Todd, she doesn't know that she's their daughter who'd been "adopted" as an infant by Judge Turpin.

11A. They were on born on "the 20th of May"—which, if the heroine of *My Fair Lady* had her way, the King would proclaim "Liza Doolittle Day."

12A. Usher is the leading character in the Tony and Pulitzer Prize–winning *A Strange Loop.*

Usher is also the name most commonly used by Usher Raymond, who in 2006 spent six weeks as Billy Flynn in *Chicago.*

13A. The line is "Screw your courage to the sticking place," which Gaston says when leading a charge against "the Beast." Angelica Schuyler sings it in "Take a Break."

The quotation comes from *Macbeth*, or "The Scottish play," depending on where you are and if you're reading this aloud.

14A. The 1959 five-performance flop *Happy Town* received a Best Choreography Tony nomination for Lee Scott (in his only Broadway job) while Jerome Robbins for *Gypsy* did not.

15A. Play the cast albums, and you'll hear these Tony-winners mentioned in those songs: 1) Tommy Tune, 2) Lauren Bacall, 3) Donna McKechnie, 4) Maggie Smith, and 5) Yul Brynner.

16A. *Annie* has a song called "Annie," but it's probably not in the overture because it simply isn't one of the score's best songs.

17A. George M. Cohan, the subject of *George M!* in 1968, led his audience to believe that he was "born on the Fourth of July." Truth to tell, he was actually born on July 3, 1878.

18A. From May 1, 2002, through December 21, 2006, the Winter Garden Theatre was known as the *Cadillac* Winter Garden.

Mamma Mia! was the tenant during those fifty-four months (and beyond).

19A. In 1965, Barbara Harris played both Daisy Gamble and Melinda Wells in *On a Clear Day You Can See Forever.*

In 1966, she played Eve, Princess Barbara, Ella, and Passionella in *The Apple Tree.*

20A. *Hello, Dolly!* and *Fiddler on the Roof,* both 1964 musicals, respectively told of Dolly Levi and Yente, each of whom was a matchmaker by trade.

21A. The original production of *Once Upon a Mattress* played the first five of those six theaters. Its 1996 revival was housed at the Broadhurst.

22A. Nathan Lane, playing Max Bialystock in *The Producers,* envisions a nice, carefree retirement in Brazil—or, as he sings it, "Rio; Rio, by the sea-o"—lines from the title song of the 1934 film *Flying Down to Rio.*

23A. Every performer who portrayed a Turnblad in *Hairspray* won a Tony.

Dick Latesssa, portraying paterfamilias Wilbur, won as Best Featured Actor in a Musical.

Harvey Fierstein, playing Edna, won as Best Actor in a Musical.

Marissa Jaret Winokur, as daughter Tracy, won as Best Actress in a Musical.

(Granted, this was a small family of three, but still, every member won.)

24A. "Marilyn Monroe" is the opening song of *Blood Brothers,* the 1992–1993 Tony-nominated Best Musical.

She was once married to Joe DiMaggio, the New York Yankee who's mentioned in *South Pacific*'s "Bloody Mary."

Her next husband, Arthur Miller, was cited in *Little Me*'s "The Truth."

25A. *Grease* held the long-run title from 1980 through 1983, when it was eclipsed by *A Chorus Line*.

In the former hit, "Look at Me, I'm Sandra Dee" has Betty Rizzo sing "As for you, Troy Donahue."

In the latter hit, "Hello Twelve, Hello Thirteen, Hello Love" has Bobby sing "If Troy Donahue could be a movie star, then I could be a movie star."

26A. "Rat-Tat-Tat-Tat" from the Broadway production of *Funny Girl* had chorines, playing doughboys, establish that they come from these states before one claimed to be Private Schwartz from Rockaway.

27A. Mississippi was the twentieth state to be admitted into the union and Kentucky the fifteenth. Merge them, and you get Missitucky, where *Finian's Rainbow* takes place.

28A. *Fifth of July* opened on Broadway not on July fifth, but on the fifth of November, 1980, a year that included a Leap Year Day.

29A. According to the women who murdered them in the musical *Chicago*, they had it comin'.

30A. No, it's not Barbra Streisand, who doesn't sing a note in "If a Girl Isn't Pretty," the opening song.

It's Jean Stapleton, who seven years later would become a household name as Edith Bunker on *All in the Family*.

31A. In Bob Randall and Stephen Schwartz's 1974 musical *The Magic Show*, Alice Cooper was mentioned in "Solid Silver Platform Shoes," Betty Crocker in "Sweet, Sweet, Sweet," Gloria Steinem in "Charmin's Lament," and Karen Horney, Jascha Heifetz, Conrad Hilton, Carlo Ponti, Levi Strauss, and Joanne Woodward in "Style."

32A. In 1973, The Andrews Sisters starred in a musical written by the Sherman Brothers: *Over Here!*

33A. *Man of La Mancha* starts with "I, Don Quixote" and then segues into "Dulcinea" and then "Aldonza."

The first song does indeed name the leading male character, while the second is the name that the Don gives the local prostitute. However, her real name is Aldonza.

34A. Patrick Dennis's novels *Little Me* and *Auntie Mame* became musicals.

The former had him as an amanuensis to would-be-legend Belle Poitrine.

The latter—simply called *Mame*—characterized him as a child in act 1 and an adult in act 2.

35A. In "A Summer in Ohio" from *The Last 5 Years,* Cathy mentions Anita, Tevye, and Porgy.

36A. *I Do! I Do!*—based on *The Fourposter*, the 1951–1952 Tony-winning Best Play—had a logo of a man and woman in just such a bed.

37A. Each mentions a college or university.

1) CCNY, 2) Princeton, 3) Columbia, 4) Oral Roberts U, 5) Harvard, 6) Yale, and 7) King's College.

38A. Those theaters still have the same names, letter for letter, that they were given when they opened.

Even the Ambassador was "The New Ambassador" for a while.

But the fourteen cited above have not changed, abridged, or enhanced their names in any way.

39A. *Baker Street*, about Sherlock Holmes, was directed (but not produced by) Harold Prince.

40A. All had Oscar-winning stars in the leads: 1) Katharine Hepburn, 2) Bette Davis, 3) Vivien Leigh, 4) Paul Lukas, 5) Jose Ferrer,

6) Shirley Booth, 7) Myoshi Umeki, 8) Shelley Winters, 9) Shirley Jones, 10) Joel Grey, and 11) F. Murray Abraham.

41A. Some months before *The Pajama Game* won the 1954–1955 Best Musical Tony Award, Hollywood producer Hal Wallis attended to see the much-acclaimed Carol Haney. Alas, Haney had fractured her ankle and was unable to perform, but Wallis stayed and was smitten with her understudy; he signed this Shirley MacLaine soon after.

This incident is mentioned in the 1969–1970 Tony-winner *Applause* in "She's No Longer a Gypsy," which deals with an understudy's success: "You got up early and pulled a Shirley MacLaine."

42A. In *Nunsense*'s "Playing Second Fiddle," Sister Robert Anne mentions, "Lenora Nemetz has it on her resume that she understudied everyone."

Add an *o* and you'll get Leonora. The 1972–1973 Tony-winning *A Little Night Music*, in "A Weekend in the Country," has Anne read on an engraved invitation "Madame Leonora Armf—oh, no!"

Oh, yes: Leonora is Madame Armfeldt's first name. She was originally played by Hermione Gingold, who lost the Tony to castmate Patricia Elliott.

43A. Jerome Weidman's 1937 novel *I Can Get It for You Wholesale* had Harry Bogen as its antihero, but the 1951 film had Susan Hayward playing the character who was renamed Harriet Boyd.

For the 1962 musical, Harry Bogen returned; Elliot Gould played him. While he was at it, he fell in love with the woman who stole the show from him: Barbra Streisand.

44A. "Hats off!"—the first words sung in *Follies*, Sondheim's 1971 musical—could spur Joanne, a character in his previous musical *Company*, to ask "Does anyone still wear a hat?"

45A. *At the Grand*, the musical that closed in San Francisco in 1958, in 1989 became *Grand Hotel*, which was the name of the novel and film on which both musicals had been based.

46A. "The Grass Is Always Greener"—meaning the title of the song that Marilyn Cooper (1934–2009) sang with Lauren Bacall in *Woman of the Year* (for which both won Tonys)—can be seen on her headstone in Mount Judah Cemetery in Ridgewood, New York.

47A. *The Phantom of the Opera* opened in January, while the others opened in successive months: *Crazy for You,* February; *Aladdin,* March; *A Strange Loop,* April; and so on.

48A. Although many have referred to those songs by those titles, they aren't the songs' official names. The actual titles are

1) "A Hymn to Him," 2) "The Good Time Girl," 3) "I'll Never Be Jealous Again," 4) "Not While I'm Around," 5) "Jeanette's Showbiz Number," and 6) "Gooch's Song."

49A. "Anatevka" opened act 2 of *Fiddler on the Roof* when it opened in Detroit; by the time it reached Broadway, it was the musical's final song.

50A. After Tessie Tura complains that her G-string "just don't bump when I do," Mazeppa tartly responds, "Maybe there's something wrong with your bumper."

(Granted, in the musical the context is substantially different from what it would be on the road.)

51A. Each song mentions Fred Astaire.

1) "You're the nimble tread of the feet of Fred Astaire," 2) "Fred Astaire once worked so hard he often lost his breath," 3) "Can he dance like Fred Astaire?" 4) "On stage: Fred Astaire," and 5) "Why, he's as graceful as Fred Astaire."

52A. "I Shall Scream" in *Oliver!* reveals that Mr. Bumble expresses a desire to be a "chubby hubby." That became the name of a Ben and Jerry's flavor in 1994.

53A. *Golden Boy* played Broadway from 1964 to 1966 and at Encores! in 2002. Given that the main character of *The Catcher in the Rye* is Holden Caulfield, if you move down the alphabet from G to H, you'd get *Holden Boy*.

54A. Producers Cy Feuer and Ernest H. Martin had hired songwriter Frank Loesser and librettist Jo Swerling for *Guys and Dolls*. Swerling didn't work out, and Abe Burrows came in and made the show into the 1950–1951 Best Musical Tony-winner.

Eleven years later, Feuer and Martin had hired songwriter Loesser and librettists Jack Weinstock and Willie Gilbert for *How to Succeed in Business Without Really Trying*. Once again, librettist Burrows came to the rescue and turned the show into the 1961–1962 Best Musical Tony-winner (and a Pulitzer Prize–winner to boot).

55A. Julie Andrews—a nominee for *My Fair Lady, Camelot,* and *Victor/Victoria* (a nomination she rejected because she was insulted that no one else in the cast was so recognized)—was born on Walton-on-Thames. She was once married to Tony Walton.

56A. None of them, despite being hits, appeared in their musical's overture.

For those who might say "*A Little Night Music* doesn't have an overture," Sondheim always insisted that it does: all that vocalizing at the beginning serves as one.

57A. Richard Rodgers, whose *Oklahoma!* set the musical long-run record with 2,212 performances, and Sheldon Harnick, whose *Fiddler on the Roof* set yet another with 3,242 performances, in 1976 wrote *Rex*.

In pig Latin, it would translate to X-ray.

58A. Their lyrics all mention sections of the theater.

1, 2, and 3) mezzanine, 4) orchestra and balcony, and 5) balcony, mezzanine, and orchestra.

59A. Georges—with an *s*—was the actual first name of Georges Seurat (1859–1891), the main character in *Sunday in the Park with George.*

Both Stephen Sondheim and James Lapine agreed that putting the *s* at the end of the familiar name would be too strange for audiences.

60A. All became Oscar-nominated films that lost the Academy Award.

61A. In September 1980, three and a half years after *Annie* had opened, Betty Hutton took over as Miss Hannigan.

Three decades earlier, however, she had succeeded Judy Garland in the film version of *Annie Get Your Gun.*

62A. Imagine how humiliated choreographer Bob Fosse would have felt if his show called *Dancin'* didn't win the Tony for Best Choreography.

But it did.

63A. Cheyenne is the capitol of Wyoming; Jackson is the capitol of Mississippi.

Cheyenne Jackson spelled Gavin Creel as Wolf and Cinderella's Prince in the 2022 revival of *Into the Woods*; he had also been the lead in *All Shook Up,* roller-skated in *Xanadu,* and was the leading man in the rather ribald *The Performers.*

64A. *Gypsy's* act 1 closer, "Everything's Coming Up Roses," has Rose sing "Now's your inning."

Near the end of act 2 with "Rose's Turn," she sings "Startin' now I bat a thousand."

65A. In *Damn Yankees,* Gwen Verdon didn't enter until five songs had already been sung by her castmates.

Ray Walston, playing the devilish Mr. Applegate, didn't sing his one and only number ("Those Were the Good Old Days") until deep in the second act.

And yet both won Tonys in the leading musical categories.

66A. Thomas Jefferson was a delegate from Virginia and not yet the third President of the United States during *1776.* He was indeed in office during *1600 Pennsylvania Avenue.*

Ken Howard portrayed him in the original casts of both musicals.

67A. *A Raisin in the Sun,* which was nominated for the 1959–1960 Best Play Tony, and *Raisin,* which won the 1973–1974 Best Musical Tony, took their titles from playwright Lorraine Hansberry's tribute to Langston Hughes's 1951 poem "Harlem."

It asked "What happens to a dream deferred? Does it dry up like a raisin in the sun?"

But it has nothing to do with what goes on in either the play or the musical.

68A. All had males in their leads who were replaced by females.

1) Lillias White played the role that had been originated by Andre De Shields, 2) Whoopi Goldberg succeeded Nathan Lane as Pseudolus, 3) Patina Miller redefined the role of the Leading Player that Ben Vereen had originated, and 4) after Tom Conti left his role as Ken Harrison, Mary Tyler Moore became Claire Harrison in the play's return engagement.

69A. "Happily Ever After" was a Mary Rodgers–Marshall Barer song in *Once Upon a Mattress,* which Carol Burnett performed for sixty-one of the musical's sixty-two-week run.

It was also the name of the song that Dean Jones sang in *Company* during the Boston run, until Sondheim and Prince replaced it with

"Being Alive." But Jones didn't sing that one very long, either, for he left the musical after a month.

70A. In 1957, Onna White choreographed *The Music Man,* which starts on July 4, 1912.

In 1969, she choreographed *1776,* which concludes on July 4, 1776.

71A. Each of the original productions had a performer with a hyphenated name.

1) Andrew Keenan-Bolger, 2) Celia Keenan-Bolger, 3) Lin-Manuel Miranda, 4) Daphne Rubin-Vega, 5) Catherine Zeta-Jones, and 6) Wilfred Hyde-White.

72A. Considering that Kiley had starred in the 1965 original production and eventually appeared in *Man of La Mancha*'s 1972 and 1977 Broadway revivals, he could have justifiably sung Elaine Stritch's line in "The Little Things You Do Together":

"I've done it three or four times."

73A. Each sings a "Soliloquy."

74A. "Me and the Sky" from *Come from Away* has Beverley mention American Airlines, which has its name on a West 42nd Street theater.

75A. All had subsequent cast albums during their runs in order to promote replacement performers.

1) and 2) Brooke Shields, 3) Vanessa Williams, and 4) Pearl Bailey.

76A. Pinocchio, a character created by Carlo Collodi in 1883, became the title character of Walt Disney's 1940 film. In it, Pinocchio sang the Leigh Harline–Ned Washington song "I've Got No Strings."

That could be said by someone who bought the album that features Richard Rodgers's 1961–1962 Tony-winning score: "I've got *No Strings.*"

77A. Charlie Brown of *Peanuts* fame is referenced in the title song of *You're a Good Man, Charlie Brown*, whose 1999 revival ran from early February to mid-June.

"Charlie Brown" was a song in *Smokey Joe's Café*, which had a 1995–2000 run.

78A. Each of them has a song that tells you where the musical takes place.

1) "N.Y.C.," 2) "Anatevka," 3) "Coney Island, U.S.A.," 4) "New York, New York," and 5) "Chicago."

79A. After appearing in the 1924 revue *I'll Say She Is*, Adolph Marx changed his first name to Harpo.

That's also the name of the character that Brandon Victor Dixon first played and Kyle Scatliffe subsequently portrayed in *The Color Purple*.

80A. They played teenagers in their musicals, and are listed in order of their characters' ages.

1) Evan in *13* is indeed thirteen. 2) Kim in *Bye Bye Birdie* reminisced about being fourteen now that she's fifteen. 3) Kim in the *Bye Bye Birdie* film reminisced about being fifteen now that she's sixteen. 4) Liesl in *The Sound of Music* is sixteen going on seventeen. 5) Kim in *Miss Saigon* establishes in her first line that she is seventeen. 6) Sandy Dumbrowski in *Grease* informs us that Danny Zuko "turned 18."

81A. In *The Fantasticks*, Tom Jones called his characters the Boy and the Girl far more often than referring to them as Matt and Luisa.

82A. In "The Baseball Game" in *Falsettos*, Mendel mentions Hank Greenberg and Sandy Koufax.

The former played for the Detroit Tigers and the Pittsburgh Pirates while the latter toiled for the Dodgers during their time in Brooklyn and Los Angeles.

83A. The film is *Grand Hotel,* the 1932 Oscar-winner and the 1989–1990 Tony-nominated musical.

In the former, Elizaveta Grusinskaya, played by Greta Garbo, said the now-immortal line "I want to be alone."

In the latter, Elizaveta Grushinskaya (note the added *h* in her surname) doesn't.

84A. Somewhere in each song, *la-la-las, dah-dah-dahs,* or *ah-ah-ahs* are used instead of genuine words.

(That's a much easier way to write lyrics, isn't it?)

85A. June in *Gypsy* is said to be a "three-foot-three bundle of dynamite" in scene 5, but she had apparently grown into a "five-foot-two bundle of dynamite" by scene 9.

86A. Carolyn Leigh was the lyricist for the 1954 musical version of *Peter Pan,* but after director-choreographer Jerome Robbins deemed that new songs were necessary, Betty Comden (along with longtime collaborator Adolph Green) arrived to buttress the score.

87A. "They're Playing Our Song" from the musical of the same name established that after Sonia Walsk had heard her boyfriend, Leon, say "Can't lovin' be fun?" she was inspired to write a song by that title.

88A. Notice that the song was described as one written by John Kander and not by John Kander and Fred Ebb. *A Family Affair* is a musical that Kander didn't do with Ebb, in which a new-to-Broadway Linda Lavin sang "Harmony."

That's also the name of Barry Manilow's musical that played the National Yiddish Theatre Folksbienne in 2022.

89A. Instead of calling his play about Wolfgang Amadeus Mozart by the more expected *Mozart* or even *Wolfgang,* Peter Shaffer opted for the composer's middle name as his title: *Amadeus.*

Had writers gone that route and chosen their subjects' middle names for their musicals, we would have had the above-named titles instead of

1) *Sondheim on Sondheim,* 2) *The Will Rogers Follies,* 3) *Jerome Robbins' Broadway,* and 4) *Sunday in the Park with George.*

90A. Alfred Drake in *Kismet* played the Poet. He later assumed the identity of Hajj, but that's not his actual name.

(Only Allah knows what it is.)

91A. Louise in *Gypsy* asks "I wonder how old I am?" Considering that the future Gypsy Rose Lee was born on January 8, 1911, that's a date from which Louise could start calculating.

92A. Terrence Mann appeared as the original Broadway Rum Tug Tugger in *Cats* (7,485 performances), as the original Broadway Javert in *Les Misérables* (6,680 performances), and as the original Beast in *Beauty and the Beast* (5,462 performances).

On screen, he appeared as Larry, Zach's assistant in *A Chorus Line* as its onstage counterpart was wending its way to 6,137 performances.

93A. Thornton Wilder's *Our Town* takes place in New Hampshire; his *The Skin of Our Teeth* is set in New Jersey; his *The Matchmaker* is located in New York.

There's only one state left that begins with "New": New Mexico. So where's the Wilder play that's set there?

94A. They all mention special days of the year, and are listed in the order in which they appear on the calendar.

1) New Year's Day, 2) Groundhog Day, 3) Easter, 4) Mother's Day, 5) Memorial Day, 6) Fourth of July, 7) Labor Day, 8) Halloween, 9) Thanksgiving, 10) Christmas Eve, 11) Christmas, and 12) New Year's Eve.

95A. Jason believes that "chess is the most beautiful thing in the world," but Mr. Price insists that shoes are.

96A. Carol Channing first played young Lorelei Lee in *Gentlemen Prefer Blondes* in 1949 and then a twenty-five years older Lorelei Lee in *Lorelei* in 1974.

Similarly speaking, Chita Rivera played a young Rose in *Bye Bye Birdie* in 1960 and then a Rose who was twenty-one years older in *Bring Back Birdie* in 1981.

97A. None of them—at least as of this writing—has ever been made into a feature film, but were instead made into TV broadcasts.

98A. The song dropped from *Gypsy* is "Nice She Ain't." In *Into the Woods*'s "I Know Things Now," Sondheim states that "Nice is different than good."

So perhaps Rose is good, after all!

99A. Chita Rivera originated the role of Anita in *West Side Story* and Velma Kelly in *Chicago*. Catherine Zeta-Jones won for her Velma on film, and Rita Moreno as well as Ariana DeBose won for their Anitas.

100A. All these characters originally had different names before they changed them.

1) Mildred Plotka, 2) Joe Boyd, 3) Gertrude Slojinksi, 4) Gregory, 5) Ephraim Ramirez, 6) Danny O'Higgins, and 7) Benjamin Barker.

101A. *Gigi.* For its Broadway production in 1973, it eschewed "Thank Heaven for Little Girls," "The Night They Invented Champagne," and the Oscar-winning title song in favor of the new ones that Lerner and Loewe wrote.

102A. All were given different titles when they were filmed.

1) *The Fugitive Kind,* 2) *The Last of the Mobile Hot Shots,* 3) *Baby Doll,* and 4) *Boom!*

103A. Dorothy Loudon was the first to play Miss Hannigan in *Annie* on Broadway and won a 1976–1977 Tony for it. In 1983, she was the first Dotty Otley in *Noises Off* on Broadway.

And yet, when Hollywood adapted these properties, Carol Burnett succeeded Loudon in both roles.

104A. In 1964, Jule Styne wrote the music for *Funny Girl,* which centered on Fanny Brice.

In 1959, he wrote the music for *Gypsy.* Sondheim wrote the lyrics for "If Momma Was Married," which included "I'm not Fanny Brice."

105A. They are the surnames that Rose in *Bye Bye Birdie* has been known to have.

When the musical opened in 1960, she started out as Rose Grant, but then someone noticed that because such an issue was made of her Spanish descent, her surname should reflect that. Hence, Alvarez.

For the 1963 film version, Rose's last name was changed to DeLeon.

106A. As Lorenz Hart reminded us in *Pal Joey,* "English people don't say clerk—they say clark." Thus, at London's Lyric Theatre, it wouldn't have rhymed with "work."

(Here's hoping that British musical theater aficionados have never heard Hart's belief that "anybody who says 'clark' is a jark.")

107A. Prez in the 1954 musical *The Pajama Game* estimated what he could buy in five years if he could receive his seven and a half cent hourly raise.

Babe Williams quickly followed with her ten- and twenty-year estimates.

108A. All of them had characters who had the Roman numeral *III* after their names.

1) Warner Huntington III, 2) Andrew Makepiece Ladd III, 3) Phil Dolan III, 4) Coalhouse Walker III, 5) Benjamin Coffin III, and 6) Rocky III.

109A. In *Hamilton,* as soon as Alexander Hamilton is introduced, he sings "Alexander Hamilton."

110A. The Lyric Theater opened on 42nd Street in 1903. Its interior was demolished in 1996 to make way for the Ford Center for the Performing Arts, which became the Hilton, which became the Foxwoods, which became—at last!—the Lyric.

111A. In each of these shows, a character who had died returned.

1) Marjorie Taylor, 2) Fantine, 3) Thuy, and 4) Angel.

112A. When Alan Jay Lerner wrote "I'm an Ordinary Man" in *My Fair Lady*—which just as easily could have been called "I Shall Never Let a Woman in My Life"—he didn't use "wife" as a rhyme.

113A. All four have a melody that is later reused with new lyrics.

1) "Goodnight, My Someone" becomes "76 Trombones," 2) "Come to Me" is repurposed as "On My Own," 3) "It Sucks to Be Me" morphs into "For Now," and 4) "You'll Be Back" returns as "What Comes Next?"

114A. The 1950 Oscar-winning *All about Eve* had a character named Lloyd Richards, who was Margo Channing's director.

By 1970, when the film's musical version *Applause* opened (and won the Best Musical Tony), an actual director named Lloyd Richards had already amassed five Broadway credits, most notably for *A Raisin in the Sun*.

Buzz Richards was the director's new moniker.

115A. Joe and Meg Boyd lived in the Maryland town known as Chevy Chase.

The actor by the same name made his off-Broadway debut in 1973 in *National Lampoon's Lemmings* before he rose to fame through *Saturday Night Live.*

116A. Leo sings that he'd like to have "lunch at Sardi's every day." Helene yearns to be "a hat-check girl . . . at Sardi's East." Indeed, from 1958 to 1968, at 123 East 54th Street, Sardi's had a sister restaurant.

117A. They're all sung by characters who have the names of cities: 1) Tulsa, 2) Dallas, and 3) Phoenix.

118A. *Seesaw* arrived at the Uris Theatre with Michele Lee and Tommy Tune in the roles that had previously been respectively played by Lainie Kazan and Bill Starr.

(Well, you were warned that it was a trick question . . .)

119A. The Shubert Organization decided that whenever any of its houses were dark, a plastic slate on its marquee would say "See a Broadway Show—Just for the Fun of It!"

The practice eventually died out. Now the plastic slates are painted black, perhaps to suggest that the house is in mourning.

120A. *Sophie,* the 1963 biomusical of Sophie Tucker, ran eight performances.

Roxie Hart mentions her in "Roxie" in *Chicago,* whose original 1975 production ran 894 performances—a drop in the proverbial bucket compared to its revival.

121A. Each of them had a sequence that was inspired by a play by William Shakespeare: 1) *King Lear,* 2) *Richard III,* 3) *Hamlet,* and 4) *Macbeth.*

122A. When *Harvey* was starting out, it was called *The Pooka*—the type of creature his overgrown rabbit was said to be.

123A. Whenever the article "a" is placed before a word that starts with a vowel, it must be upped to "an." "It's a Scandal! It's *a* Outrage!" from *Oklahoma!* is missing an *n* on the article.

124A. *Arsenic and Old Lace* concerns the Brewster Sisters, who rent rooms to transients. Should they discover that the boarder has no living relatives, they feel so bad for him they euthanize him with poisoned elderberry wine and bury him in the cellar.

They've done in twelve men, so, just for fun, the 1986 revival hired a dozen actors to emerge through the cellar door during curtain calls to get one final laugh from the audience.

125A. Each of those characters hails from a New England state.

1) Connecticut; specifically, Upson Downs, 2) Maine (David even sings a song by that name), 3) Massachusetts (where you're now allowed to chop up your momma or your poppa), 4) New Hampshire (Bartlett was the Continental Congress delegate), 5) Rhode Island, where Lola was once, by her own admission, Providence's ugliest woman, and 6) Vermont, before her big day in New York.

126A. Cyrano de Bergerac, we're told, killed a hundred men all by himself—and that doesn't include Montfleury, the actor we did see him stab to death.

127A. In "Nowadays," the eleven o'clock number in *Chicago*, Roxie Hart and Velma Kelly sing, "You can even marry Harry but mess around with Ike."

Those just happen to be the first names of our thirty-third president and the nickname of our thirty-fourth.

128A. Composer Jule Styne certainly centered on musicals with locales around the United States, but *Darling of the Day*, his 1968 musical, was set in England—where indeed he was born on December 31, 1905.

129A. Rodgers and Hart's "Blue Moon" was on Presley's first album, was a number one hit for the Marcels in 1961, and was the song to which three greasers in *Grease* each showed his *gluteus maximus* during a school dance.

130A. The shows are in the order of the number of performances they ran on Broadway, from zero for *Breakfast at Tiffany's* and one for *Kelly* all the way to nine for *Anyone Can Whistle* to ten for *Tommy Tune Tonite!*

131A. "Grand Old Ivy" from the Pulitzer Prize–winning *How to Succeed in Business Without Really Trying* starts with the words "Groundhog! Groundhog!"

Such an excited response would be apt for people in Pennsylvania, where every February 2, Groundhog Day takes place in Punxsutawney.

132A. Both have important male characters whose first name is the same as his last name.

Lolita, My Love has Humbert Humbert and *The Cradle Will Rock* has Mister Mister (who is not to be confused with the rock group of the same name).

133A. Four years after Lee Marvin starred in the movie version of *Paint Your Wagon,* he appeared in the film version of Eugene O'Neill's *The Iceman Cometh.*

Costar Clint Eastwood would later direct the film of *Jersey Boys.*

Their costar Jean Seberg was the subject of *Jean,* the musical Marvin Hamlisch did with Christopher Adler (Richard's son) that played four months of the 1983–1984 season at London's National Theatre.

134A. Those words were listed first in the title of each revue followed by the word "Follies," which, needless to say, was a Sondheim musical.

1) *Broadway Follies,* 2) *Cape Cod Follies,* 3) *Grand Street Follies,* 4) *Greenwich Village Follies,* 5) *London Follies,* and 6) *Provincetown Follies.*

135A. After Dick Van Dyke won a 1960–1961 Best Featured Actor in a Musical Tony for *Bye Bye Birdie,* he starred in *The Dick Van Dyke Show.*

Two characters in the show were Buddy and Sally, which are the names of a married couple in *Follies.*

In that same musical, the character Phyllis had a maiden name of Rogers, which was Sally's surname on the television show.

136A. Each mentions a classical composer.

1) "While Verdi turned 'round in his grave," 2) "I like Offenbach," 3) "All of that Puccini going to waste," 4) "Mozart was crazy."

137A. The theater is the Music Box, which is a prop during "No More Candy" in the 1963–1964 Tony-nominated *She Loves Me.*

138A. In *Company,* Joanne and Larry in the opening title song sing "Bob, we're having people in Saturday night"—and *Saturday Night* was indeed the title of a previous Sondheim musical, although it wasn't produced until decades later.

139A. Barbara Harris, in the second act of *The Apple Tree,* played a character named Barbara—but because she was the barbarian princess (in *The Lady or the Tiger?*), the name was pronounced Bar-*bare*-uh.

140A. All have characters who are juniors.

1) Joseph Taylor Jr.; 2) Enoch Snow Jr.; 3) Curtis Taylor Jr.; 4) Joseph Kennedy Jr.; 5) Buddy Young Jr.; 6) Coalhouse Walker Jr.; and 7) Will Rogers Jr.

141A. Dolly Levi had a line early in *Hello, Dolly!* where she said "Just leave everything to me."

Although recent Oscar-nominee Carol Channing's first song had been "I Put My Hand In," Jerry Herman replaced it to have recent Oscar-winner Barbra Streisand start the film with "Just Leave Everything to Me."

142A. Both Tony-winning Best Musical *Avenue Q* in "Mix Tape," and Tony-nominated (and MTV broadcast) *Legally Blonde* in "Omigod, You Guys" mention the 1997 film *Titanic*.

It won eleven Oscars to *Avenue Q*'s three Tonys and *Legally Blonde*'s none.

143A. The person who directed the film had also directed the original stage version.

1) Harold Prince, 2) Gene Saks, 3) Morton DaCosta, 4) Peter Hunt, 5) Bob Fosse, and 6) George Abbott.

144A. All played other-worldly beings in musicals.

1) Elvira (*High Spirits*), 2) Genie (*Aladdin*), 3) Teen Angel (*Grease*), 4) Frumah Sarah (*Fiddler on the Roof*), and 5) Og (*Finian's Rainbow*).

145A. In the original cast of each musical was a performer who had appeared or would appear in the 1958 film version of *The Matchmaker*.

1) Shirley Booth: Dolly, 2) Paul Ford: Vandergelder, 3) Anthony Perkins: Cornelius, 4) Shirley MacLaine: Irene, and 5) Robert Morse: Barnaby.

146A. Before the barbershop quartet sings "Sincere," "Goodnight, Ladies," "It's You," and "Lida Rose," Harold Hill seduces them into singing the words "ice cream."

That's part of the title of "Vanilla Ice Cream," the song that Barbara Cook—the Tony-winning original Marian the Librarian in the 1957 production of *The Music Man*—sang in the 1963 musical *She Loves Me*.

147A. Each has a song that includes the value of a coin.

1) "A Penny in My Pocket, 2) "Buffalo Nickel Photoplay, Inc.," 3) "Life Turns on a Dime," and 4) "Quarter in the Bleach Cup."

148A. Harry Belafonte was the Best Featured Actor in a Musical Tony-winner in 1953–1954 for *John Murray Anderson's Almanac.*

He was the first to sell a million long-playing records as a result of his album *Calypso* (which is not to be confused with the Greek mythological character of the same name).

149A. 1) "The Rumor" has townspeople making error upon error when they relate what happened to Tevye and his family.

2) Starbuck in "Melisande" tells Lizzie about King Hamlet; as we know, Hamlet didn't live to see the day when he became king.

3) Lucy Van Pelt in "Little Known Facts" gives Linus one mistaken explanation after another with her usual unshakable certainly, and

4) Dr. Gilman tells Kate that "Shakespeare Lied" in saying that Romeo didn't commit suicide after Juliet's death.

150A. In 1980, *Barnum* had Jenny Lind sing in Swedish a song that translated to "Love Makes Such Fools of Us All."

The 1990 British cult musical *Moby Dick* (which Orson Welles had dramatized as a 1962 play) has a song called "Love Will Always (Try to Make Fools of Us All)."

151A. The song that Streisand recorded was that very song: "Better." Alas, she didn't release it for decades, many years after Kleban had died.

152A. Each musical used "gay" in the old-world sense—meaning "lighthearted and carefree" as opposed to "homosexual."

Candide did so in "Glitter and Be Gay."

Me and Juliet had a song entitled "Keep It Gay" (which is not to be confused with the song of the same name in *The Producers,* where the meaning *did* refer to homosexuality).

The early 1960s musical is *The Gay Life,* which dealt with a most heterosexual rakehell in Vienna in 1904.

153A. George S. Kaufman famously said, "Satire is what closes on Saturday night"—for that's when Broadway shows routinely shuttered.

Monday performances eventually gave way to Sunday matinees, so today Kaufman would say "Satire is what closes on Sunday afternoon."

154A. The more obvious one is Sir Edward Ramsey, the British emissary to Siam.

The other, however, is Anna Leonowens, for Lady Thiang, when first meeting this "scientific English teacher," believes the correct term of address is "Sir."

155A. Capitol not only released them as single long-playing records, but also bundled them all together in a three-record box set, although each had nothing in common with the other two.

156A. Meredith Willson for the *The Music Man,* titled his opening number "Rock Island"—words that aren't found in the song itself.

The Unsinkable Molly Brown's opening number "I Ain't Down Yet" has those words appear in dialogue that precede the song, but they're not actually in the song.

157A. Jerry Bock and Sheldon Harnick resumed collaborating after a decades-long hiatus to write "Topsy-Turvy" for the 2004 Broadway revival of *Fiddler on the Roof.*

Topsy-Turvy is also the name of the 1999 film biography of musical theater pioneers Sir William Gilbert and Sir Arthur Sullivan.

158A. Julie Andrews and Carol Burnett appeared together in *Julie and Carol at Carnegie Hall* in 1962, *Julie and Carol at Lincoln Center* in 1971, and *Julie and Carol: Together Again* in 1989.

However, they did not appear together in *Putting It Together*; Andrews did it at the Manhattan Theatre Club in 1993 and Carol Burnett took it to the Ethel Barrymore Theatre in 1999.

159A. All bested Stephen Sondheim's music and/or lyrics for the Best Score Tony via *Fiddler on the Roof* (Bock and Harnick), *A Chorus Line* (Hamlisch and Kleban), *La Cage aux Folles* (Herman), and *Nine* (Yeston).

160A. The song "Oklahoma!" as well as the 1943 musical *Oklahoma!* ended with an exclamation point.

But in the 2005 musical *Dirty Rotten Scoundrels,* a question mark ended the song called "Oklahoma?"

161A. In *Call Me Madam,* Irving Berlin's Tony-winning score, the opening number, "Mrs. Sally Adams," includes the words "God Bless America." Berlin wrote it in 1918 but had kept it in his trunk for decades.

162A. In *Flower Drum Song*—Rodgers and Hammerstein's take on venerable Chinese traditions versus new-fangled American ones— young and very Americanized Wang San meets the just as Americanized Linda Low and asks her if she knows the song "You Be the Rock, I'll Be the Roll."

"Sure!" she responds before singing, "You be the rock, I'll be the roll! You be the soup, I'll be the bowl! You be the furnace, I'll be the coal! Rock, rock, rock."

(It seemed like a good idea at the time.)

163A. When *Shenandoah* opened at The Goodspeed Opera House in East Haddam, Connecticut, in the fall of 1974, it was titled *Shenandoah, The Only Home I Know* because of its act 2 song of the same name.

164A. After Henrik sang in "Later" that he felt "all dammed up inside," he begged our pardon, because he'd said the equivalent of "damn," which he deemed profane.

Thus he wouldn't have approved of songs that state 1) "Now ain't that too damn bad," 2) "You do give a damn," 3) "We'll be damn fools a lot," 4) "Damn few," 5) "I could start to scream against the whole damn south," and 6) "Damn! Damn! Damn! Damn!"

Needless to say, he wouldn't have been fond of *Damn Yankees,* either.

165A. All have a song that is sung in another language.

1) "The Bugle" is in Dutch; 2) "Il Mondo Era Vuoto" is in Italian; 3) "Love Makes Such Fools of Us All" is in Swedish, and, for that matter, 4) all of *Rugantino* is in Italian.

166A. *Do Re Mi*—because its plot involved one Hubie Cram who endeavored to enter the jukebox business.

PART TWO

ANSWERS

TRY JUST A LITTLE BIT HARDER

167A. Each song mentions one of the earth's continents.

1) North America, 2) South America, 3) Europe, 4) Antarctica, 5) Asia, 6) Australia, and 7) Africa.

168A. "A Certain Girl" from Kander and Ebb's 1968 *The Happy Time* was sung by David Wayne, who'd already won a Tony for *Finian's Rainbow.*

Robert Goulet would win one for this musical.

Michael Rupert would win his Tony many years later for *Sweet Charity.*

169A. Given that those who perform those songs do some whistling in them, it would suggest that "Anyone can whistle"—the title of Sondheim's 1964 song and shortest-running musical.

170A. David Edward Byrd who designed the best logo ever—for *Follies*—was born on April 4, 1941—thirty years to the day before the landmark musical opened.

171A. When *Abie's Irish Rose* closed in 1927 after 2,327 performances, it was Broadway's longest-running play. (Even now, it's only slipped to third place.)

In 1925, during the play's mammoth run, Lorenz Hart, Rodgers's lyricist at the time, mentioned it in "Manhattan" in *The Garrick Gaieties:* "Our future babies we'll take to *Abie's Irish Rose.*"

Forty-six years later, Stephen Sondheim, with whom Rodgers collaborated on *Do I Hear a Waltz?*, included it in his list song "I'm Still Here" in *Follies:* "I've been through *Abie's Irish Rose.*"

172A. Arthur Miller just happens to be the name of a character in Eugene O'Neill's 1933 comedy *Ah, Wilderness!*

173A. In 1960, Bobby Darin's rendition of "Mack the Knife" hit number one and won the Grammy for Best Record of the Year.

It was the opening number of the Weill/Brecht musical *The Threepenny Opera,* which made its Broadway debut on April 13, 1933, but closed after only twelve performances.

(We think of *Threepenny* as a successful musical, but it wasn't a hit in America until its 1954 off-Broadway revival.)

174A. All of these musicals played theaters that have since been razed (more's the pity).

Kiss Me, Kate opened at The New Century Theatre.

Kismet played its entire run at the Ziegfeld Theatre.

Man of La Mancha started its long run at the ANTA-Washington Square Theatre.

My Fair Lady's Mark Hellinger hasn't been destroyed, but it's been lost in a different way, as we well know.

175A. In 1963, the first act of *Hello, Dolly!* originally ended with Mr. Vandergelder (David Burns) singing about his steady rise to wealth in "A Penny in My Pocket,"

Then "Before the Parade Passes By" replaced it.

For the 2017 revival, however, the second act began with Vandergelder (David Hyde Pierce) stepping through the part in the curtains and singing the song.

176A. Each musical contains a song that is a quodlibet.

(Don't know the term? The *Collins English Dictionary* describes it as "a humorous composition consisting of two or more independent and harmonically complementary melodies . . . played or sung together . . . in a polyphonic arrangement.")

In those above-named musicals, the quodlibets are 1) "You're Just in Love," 2) "Empty Pockets Filled with Love," 3) "You're Gonna Love Tomorrow/Love Will See Us Through," 4) "All for the Best," 5) "One Step," 6) "Lounging at the Waldorf," 7) "Gaugin's Shoes," and 8) "My Dream for Tomorrow."

177A. *Damn Yankees* was based on *The Year the Yankees Lost the Pennant* by Douglass Wallop, which he cowrote with George Abbott. It starred Stephen Douglass.

Usually, the name is spelled "Douglas," as is the case with Douglas Hodge, who won the 2009–2010 Best Actor in a Musical Tony for the revival of *La Cage aux Folles*.

178A. *Dames at Sea*'s leading lady, Bernadette Peters, won her first Tony in 1986 for *Song & Dance*, a dozen years after her understudy Janie Sell had won for *Over Here!*

179A. Miss Adelaide, played by the Tony-nominated Vivian Blaine; Princess Winnifred, portrayed by the Tony-nominated Carol Burnett; and Angelica Schuyler, played by Tony-winner Renee Elise Goldsberry, all liked to read.

Adelaide consults a book on psychology in "Adelaide's Lament."

Winnifred reads a fairy tale in "Happily Ever After."

Angelica sings in "The Schuyler Sisters" that she's read Thomas Paine's *Common Sense*.

180A. Stephen Schwartz's first hit was *Godspell,* which gets a production in Indiana in *The Prom.*

181A. In "So Long, Dearie," Channing and Streisand informed Horace that "I'm gonna learn to dance and smoke a cigarette."

Martin and Bailey apparently noticed—or did songwriter Jerry Herman or someone else?—that Dolly obviously *had* learned to dance, for earlier in the musical she had taught Cornelius and Barnaby to do just that.

Martin and Bailey opted for "hoochy-kooch" instead.

182A. *Jimmy*—the biomusical about New York City Mayor James J. Walker (1881–1946)—opened in October 1969.

It was soon followed in December 1969 by *Coco*—the biomusical about famed fashion designer Gabrielle "Coco" Chanel.

Put them together, and you get Jimmy Coco, which is what friends of James Coco, star of Neil Simon's *Last of the Red Hot Lovers,* affectionately called him.

183A. The synonym for "twilight" is "crepuscule," which was the title of a play—with each letter separated by dashes—that was adapted into *The 25th Annual Putnam County Spelling Bee.*

184A. Each Tony-losing musical of those seasons went on to become an Oscar-winning film: *West Side Story* (1961), *Oliver!* (1968), and *Chicago* (2002).

But each Tony-winning musical of those seasons had a film version that didn't: *The Music Man* (1961), *A Funny Thing Happened on the Way to the Forum* (1963), and *A Chorus Line* (1985).

185A. All mention a soft drink.

1) Pepsi-Cola, 2) Dr. Pepper, 3) 7-Up, and 4) Coke.

186A. The film was *The Blob.* For *Merrily We Roll Along,* Sondheim wrote a song called "The Blob."

187A. "When She Comes in the Room," from Dorothy Fields's 1945 five hundred–performance musical *Up in Central Park,* may or may not have crossed Jerry Herman's mind when he wrote "When Mabel Comes in the Room" for *Mack & Mabel,* his short-running 1974 musical.

188A. In *Mack & Mabel,* Mabel Normand sings in "Look What Happened to Mabel" that "Miss Avenue R is a regalar [*sic*] star."

(Extra credit if you also knew that Rosie of *Really Rosie* fame lives one block north on Avenue P.)

189A. To be frank, "pinkel" is the German word for "pee." "Stadt" translates to "city."

Translation: *Urinetown.*

190A. Considering the occupation of the leading character of the 1979 musical *The Best Little Whorehouse in Texas* (with Best Featured Actress in a Musical Tony-winner Carlyn Glynn), that musical could just as easily have had the name of the 1950 musical *Call Me Madam* (which starred Best Actress in a Musical Tony-winner Ethel Merman).

191A. All were based on Pulitzer Prize–winning plays.

1) *Look Homeward, Angel,* 2) *Idiot's Delight,* 3) *Picnic,* 4) *They Knew What They Wanted,* 5) *Anna Christie,* 6) *Harvey,* 7) *Street Scene,* 8) *The Diary of Anne Frank,* and 9) *The Teahouse of the August Moon.*

192A. In 1981, the three-performance flop *Oh, Brother!* had a song called "It's a Man's World."

In 2000, *The Full Monty* ran for a hit-making 770 performances with an opening number that had a group of women insisting that "It's a Woman's World."

193A. Pop star Sergio Franchi starred in *Do I Hear a Waltz?* by no less than Richard Rodgers, Stephen Sondheim, and Arthur Laurents. It opened in March 1965 and lasted 220 performances.

In March 1966, Franchi's sister, Dana Valery, opened *Wait a Minim,* a South African revue. It may be forgotten now and its cast album may never be officially transferred to CD, but it lasted 456 performances—more than twice as long as *Do I Hear a Waltz?*

194A. Each has a song with a title that includes the days of the week.

1) "Sunday Morning Fever," 2) "Mine Till Monday," 3) "Terrible Tuesday," 4) "Wednesday's Growing Up," 5) "Sweet Thursday," 6) "Friday Night Jackson," and 7) "Saturday Night in the City."

195A. "Baby, Talk to Me" was in the 1960–1961 Tony-winning *Bye Bye Birdie.*

"Talk to Me, Baby" was in the 1964 flop *Foxy,* for which Bert Lahr won a Tony.

Frank Sinatra recorded it, but so did Jesse Pearson—Conrad Birdie in *Bye Bye Birdie's* 1963 film.

196A. Throughout Arthur Laurents's book, he spells the diminutive for mother as "Momma." Notice, too, that "If Momma Was Married" is the official name of the song.

So at the very least, Mrs. Hovick would be Momma Rose.

197A. *Silk Stockings'* title song had both music and lyrics by Cole Porter when it played Broadway. When Hollywood filmed it, however, Cyd Charisse simply danced to the melody while caressing her newest purchase.

198A. In 1971, in "Don't Look at Me" from *Follies,* Benjamin Stone said, "What we need is a drink."

In the 1987 London production, Sondheim changed it.

(Why? Don't look at me.)

199A. When bookwriter Thomas Meehan was writing *Annie,* he decided that the lass would be born on October 28 in honor of his own daughter's birthday.

But Harold Gray, who authored and drew the famous comic strip, then said Annie came into this world on Leap Year Day.

"Leap" is the first syllable of Annie's favorite expression: "Leapin' lizards!"

200A. *Do Re Mi* reversed its colors for its 1965 reissue.

201A. During the 1970s, Boris Aronson designed five musicals with Stephen Sondheim scores and Harold Prince's direction. He died on November 16, 1980—precisely one year to the day before Sondheim and Prince's poorly reviewed *Merrily We Roll Along* opened.

202A. For more than ten thousand performances, Velma Kelly sang "I betcha Lucky Lindy never flew so high"—meaning Charles Lindbergh—in *Chicago*'s "All That Jazz," by John Kander and Fred Ebb.

In the team's 1997 flop *Steel Pier,* Rita Racine was known as "Lindy's Lovebird," because she was the first person to kiss Lindbergh when he returned to America after his solo transatlantic flight.

203A. In Sondheim's *Anyone Can Whistle,* a group of unbalanced individuals are dubbed "Cookies."

In his next musical, *Do I Hear a Waltz?,* lead character Leona affectionately calls her ten-year-old tour guide "Cookie."

204A. Charles Strouse and Lee Adams wrote *"It's a Bird . . . It's a Plane . . . It's Superman"* in 1966, but weren't allowed to use the DC Comics characters Jimmy Olsen, Lana Lang, Lex Luthor, and Mr. Mxyzlptk.

In 1970 when they wrote *Applause,* the musical version of *All about Eve,* they were restricted from using Addison DeWitt, Birdie Coonan, Max Fabian, and Miss Casswell.

205A. *Uncle Tom Cabin*'s villain was Simon Legree.

When Tuptim adapted it as *The Small House of Uncle Thomas* (in *The King and I*), she dubbed him Simon *of* Legree.

206A. Elaine May, who costarred at the Golden Theatre in 1960 as half of *An Evening with Mike Nichols and Elaine May*, returned there and gave a Tony-winning performance in *The Waverly Gallery* in 2018.

Her "first and only reviewed Broadway appearance as a performer" was specified, not only because she'd been reviewed as a Broadway playwright on three separate occasions, but also because she did appear in a Broadway play called *The Office* in 1966 that closed during previews and therefore wasn't reviewed.

207A. Oscar Wilde's 1895 masterpiece *The Importance of Being Earnest* was musicalized in 1960 as *Ernest in Love*.

Notice, though, that in the play, "Earnest" is an adjective spelled with an *a* and in the musical, "Ernest" is a proper noun spelled without an *a*.

208A. In Cole Porter's score for *Kiss Me, Kate*, Lois sings "Always true to you, darling, in my fashion."

However, "darling" is not part of the song's title, which actually is "Always True to You in My Fashion."

209A. Sondheim originally envisioned that *Follies* would include "All Things Bright and Beautiful," but it never got as far as Boston.

In 1975, *Chicago* still had "Loopin' the Loop" in Philadelphia, but parted company with it before Broadway.

210A. *Up* was the name of the musical that was to open at the Uris Theatre. However, some people feared that theatergoers would read the marquee as "*Up* Uris."

So the musical became *Via Galactica* at the theater that only much later became The Gershwin.

211A. All played more than one role in the productions that won them Tonys.

1) *The Rothschilds,* 2) *City of Angels,* 3) *Stop the World—I Want to Get Off,* 4) *Peter Pan,* 5) *Oh! What a Lovely War,* 6) *Jerome Robbins' Broadway,* and 7) *A Funny Thing Happened on the Way to the Forum.*

(Did you remember that Pseudolus also plays a character called Prologus?)

212A. Paula Stewart, who sang "Hey, Look Me Over!" with Lucille Ball in *Wildcat,* was once married to Burt Bacharach, who composed the music for *Promises, Promises.* It lost the Best Musical Tony to *1776.*

213A. When Columbia Records first issued *Camelot,* Richard Burton and Julie Andrews were above the title.

After fifth-billed Robert Goulet became famous in his own right (he's even mentioned in *A Chorus Line*) and became a Tony-winner himself (for *The Happy Time*), he became the third name above the title on subsequent reissues.

214A. Barbara Barrie opened in *Company* in April 1970. Hal Linden opened in *The Rothschilds* that October. Both musicals closed on January 1, 1972.

In 1974, Linden took the title role in TV's *Barney Miller.* A year later, joining him as his wife on the series was Barrie.

Barrie was married to Jay Harnick, whose brother Sheldon wrote the lyrics to *The Rothschilds.*

215A. Gene Kelly was the leading man of *Pal Joey* in 1940 while Stanley Donen was in the ensemble.

They'd eventually codirect the film *Singin' in the Rain* in 1952, which became a Broadway musical in 1985.

216A. "Ain't Misbehavin'," by composers Thomas "Fats" Waller and Harry Brooks with lyrics by Andy Razaf, is the name of both the song and the 1977–1978 Tony-winning musical.

217A. Liat in *South Pacific* has a mere five lines. She mostly "spoke" with her hands.

218A. Donna McKechnie, who won the Tony for her Cassie in *A Chorus Line,* does not have an *a* in her last name. Eulalie Mackechnie Shinn of *The Music Man* does.

219A. Diana Ross, who was born on March 26, 1944, recorded with The Supremes an album of songs from *Funny Girl,* which opened on Broadway on March 26, 1964.

220A. Ginger Rogers was the leading lady of the 1956 film *The First Traveling Saleslady,* which also starred Carol Channing.

Eight years later, Channing starred in *Hello, Dolly!* until Rogers succeeded her.

221A. *Oklahoma!* played all of its 2,212 performances at the St. James.

South Pacific enjoyed 1,712 of its 1,925 performances at the Majestic before it moved to the Broadway Theatre.

The Sound of Music played 1,232 of its 1,443 performances at the Lunt-Fontanne before it moved to the late, lamented Mark Hellinger Theatre.

And finally, racking up 1,147 performances at the Imperial Theatre was *Annie Get Your Gun.*

True, Irving Berlin, and Herbert and Dorothy Fields wrote *Annie Get Your Gun*—but Rodgers and Hammerstein *produced* it. That was more than enough to get their names in the *Playbill.*

222A. The song is "My Kind of Town" from the 1964 film *Robin and the Seven Hoods.*

The kind of town is Chicago, which Robin mentions ten times before adding that it has "all that jazz."

Those last three words are, of course, part of the title of the opening number of *Chicago*: "And All That Jazz."

223A. "Pretty Lady" from the 1976 musical *Pacific Overtures* is also the name of the fictitious musical in the 1980 hit *42nd Street*.

224A. All have songs whose titles mention an alcoholic beverage.

1) "Seven Sheep, Four Red Shirts, and a Bottle of Gin," 2) "Molasses to Rum," 3) "Give Me a Pigfoot and a Bottle of Beer," 4) "Cocktail Counterpoint," 5) "Hand Me the Wine and the Dice," and 6) "Champagne."

225A. In *Milk and Honey*, Jerry Herman—soon to be famous for *Hello, Dolly!* and *Mame*—wrote the song "Chin Up, Ladies!"

In it, Clara (Molly Picon) urged the widows with whom she was traveling to "Climb ev'ry mountain to find your Mr. Snow"—references to songs in *The Sound of Music* and *Carousel*.

226A. The 1956–1957 Tonys were given to only three musicals.

My Fair Lady, which won six, has a song "Just You Wait."

Bells Are Ringing, which won two, has "Just in Time."

Li'l Abner, which also won two, has "Jubilation T. Cornpone."

227A. When you upgraded from four houses, you could point to a certain red piece of plastic and sing a song from *On Your Toes*: "There's a Small Hotel."

228A. "Aquarius" from *Hair*. The intermediate stop, by the way, was at a now-long-gone discotheque called Cheetah.

229A. *Oh! Calcutta!*—a revue that was infamous for its almost curtain-to-curtain nudity and sexually provocative sketches—was then in the sixth year of a revival that would last for thirteen years and 5,959 performances.

230A. In "Haven't the Words," there's a mention of Sweeney Todd and his razor—nine years before he'd become the subject of a Tony-winning musical.

(Remember, Sweeney Todd was a well-known character in British literature and folklore long before Sondheim discovered him.)

231A. Voltaire wrote the novel *Candide* in 1759.

George Bernard Shaw wrote *Candida* 1894.

The musical version of *Candide* debuted in 1956.

232A. Mr. Kringelein appears in only one scene in *Gypsy,* but his namesake has much more to do in *Grand Hotel,* for which Michael Jeter won a Tony.

233A. At least one of the musical's writers was part of the original cast.

1) Gerome Ragni and James Rado, 2) Lin-Manuel Miranda, 3) Peter Allen, 4) Gretchen Cryer, 5) Stew, and 6) and 7) Anthony Newley.

234A. In the 1952–1953 Tony-winning musical *Wonderful Town*, Tony-winner Rosalind Russell, playing Ruth Sherwood, sang "Swing!"

Its lyrics include, "Rock and roll to the beat-beat-beat of Speedy Valenti and his Krazy Kats."

235A. All allude to *My Fair Lady.*

1) "It was good to know I could grow unaccustomed to your face!"; 2) "By George, I think you've got it!"; 3) "She's an ordinary girl!"; and 4) "I saw *My Fair Lady.* I sort of enjoyed it."

236A. Rudy Vallee, who appeared in *How to Succeed in Business Without Really Trying* both on stage and on film, is mentioned in "That's How Young I Feel" from the Tony-nominated *Mame.*

237A. In early 1962, Anita Gillette in *All American* played a college student who sang in "Nightlife" that she wanted "to Twist until I get arrested!"

In late 1962, in *Mr. President*, Gillette sang Irving Berlin's "The Washington Twist."

238A. No, it's not "Supercalifragilisticexpialidocious" the thirty-four-letter word from *Mary Poppins*.

It's not "Mississississississississinnewah," the name of the river in the song that Ethel Merman and Paula Laurence did in the 1943 musical *Something for the Boys*. That has only thirty letters in it, little more than half the length of a word with no fewer than fifty-eight letters:

Llanfairpwllgwyngyllgogerychwyrndrobwllllantysiliogogogoch.

It's the unwieldy name of the town in Wales that's the last word in "The Boy from . . . ," music by Mary Rodgers, lyrics by Stephen Sondheim, originally written for the 1966 revue *The Mad Show*.

239A. In *Flower Drum Song*, Pat Suzuki was cast in a leading role, and Jack Suzuki in a much smaller one. For her sake, he changed his surname to Soo.

When the film was made, Nancy Kwan succeeded Suzuki, but Jack Soo was promoted to the secondary male lead.

240A. Barbara Hutton—Barbara Woolworth Hutton, in fact—had no fewer than seven husbands. So as George Furth and Stephen Sondheim were writing *Merrily We Roll Along*, they originally titled the musical that Franklin Shepard and Charley Kringas were writing *Musical Husbands: The Barbara Hutton Story*.

As the show got closer to production, Sondheim and Furth may have thought that omitting a reference to her would be in better taste.

241A. Irving Berlin, who won the Best Score Tony for *Call Me Madam,* was born Israel Baline: *B-a-l-i-n-e*.

That's an anagram for Blaine—*B-l-a-i-n-e*—as in Vivian Blaine, who appeared in *Guys and Dolls* that same season.

(And does anyone think *that* score should have lost to *Call Me Madam*? This must have been a type of Lifetime Achievement award for Berlin, for all of his previous shows had been produced before the Tonys began.)

242A. The song from the Tony-winning *Bye Bye Birdie* is "Kids!" in which the harried Mr. McAfee laments about teenagers.

Albert and his mother, Mae, weren't in the number on Broadway, but in the 1963 film, they were. At the start of this version, Albert is planning to marry Rosie, but by the end, he's reneged and says he won't—thus moving the action forward as Rosie goes forward to find another man.

243A. *Carousel* was 1) the only one of Rodgers and Hammerstein's films not to receive at least one Oscar nomination, 2) the only one told in flashback and, 3) the only one in which a lead left during filming and had to be replaced: Frank Sinatra by Gordon MacRae.

244A. *Sweet Charity,* first produced in 1966, revived in 1986, and revived again in 2005, starts with Charity in love with Charley. But the script and the *Playbill* for the first two productions only refer to him as Dark Glasses, for that's what he wears.

Only in 2005 was he given the nickname in all the printed material.

245A. *The Wiz* is the 1974–1975 Tony-winning musical. In 1964 Sondheim wrote "Come Play Wiz Me" for Fay, a character pretending to be French, in his *Anyone Can Whistle*.

246A. *Man of La Mancha* opened at the since-razed ANTA Washington Square on West 4th Street.

It then moved uptown to the Martin Beck, which is now the Al Hirschfeld.

Then it returned downtown to the Eden on Second Avenue, which is now a multiplex.

Finally, it went uptown to the Mark Hellinger, which is now, sad to say, a church.

247A. *Gypsy* is the 1950s Tony-nominated musical that mentioned the three people in the lyrics "Santa Claus is sitting here" ("Mr. Goldstone"), "Said this bum'll be Beau Brummel," and "Astaire bit!" (both in "All I Need Is the Girl").

Annie is the multiple Tony-winning musical that mentions them in "Santa Claus we never see; Santa Claus? What's that? Who's he?" ("It's the Hard-Knock Life"), "Your clothes may be Beau Brummel-y" ("You're Never Fully Dressed without a Smile"), and "Like Fred and Adele, they're walking on air now" ("I Don't Need Anything but You").

248A. For the 1966 musical *The Apple Tree*, Harnick wrote a song called "In Gaul," which referred to the country most remembered from Julius Caesar's *Commentaries on the Gallic War*.

249A. In the years after the 1936 publication and 1939 film version of *Gone with the Wind*, a joke emerged where the final word was pronounced as "whynd."

Thus Lorenz Hart, in *Babes in Arms*'s "The Lady Is a Tramp," rhymed "behind" and "mind" with *Gone with the Whynd*.

Cole Porter, in *Kiss Me, Kate*'s "Where Is the Life That Late I Led?" had Petruchio ask "Where is the fun I used to find? Where is it now? Gone with the whynd."

250A. Marilyn Monroe did the movie versions of the Broadway hits *Gentlemen Prefer Blondes*, *The Seven Year Itch*, and *Bus Stop* as well as the Broadway flop *The Sleeping Prince* (which for film was renamed *The Prince and the Showgirl*).

Her third husband was Arthur Miller, so had she taken his name, she would have become Marilyn Miller, whom Broadway audiences in the 1920s knew from her hits *Sally* and *Sunny*.

251A. *Someone's Coming Hungry* opened on March 31, 1969, starring Blythe Danner, who'd win a Tony the following year for *Butterflies Are Free*.

Danner caught the eye of coproducer Bruce Paltrow; they married and gave birth to a daughter named Gwyneth, who won the Oscar in 1999 for *Shakespeare in Love*.

252A. On stage, *Bye Bye Birdie* offers "An English Teacher," "Heathy Normal American Boy," and "Spanish Rose."

On screen, it does not.

253A. Temple Texas was one of the ladies of the evening in *Pipe Dream*, Rodgers and Hammerstein's 1955 effort.

Temple, Texas, exists—sixty-five miles north of Austin: population 78,439.

254A. They all mention Oscar-winning actors in the chronological order of their wins.

1) Gary Cooper (*Sergeant York,* 1941; *High Noon,* 1952), 2) Marlon Brando (*On the Waterfront,* 1954; *The Godfather,* 1972), 3) Yul Brynner (*The King and I,* 1956), 4) David Niven (*Separate Tables,* 1958), 5) John Wayne (*True Grit,* 1969), 6) Jane Fonda (*Klute*), and 7) Jodie Foster (*The Accused,* 1988; *Silence of the Lambs,* 1991).

255A. This is the sequence of the first one-word title to the first five-word title.

1) *Kismet,* 2) *South Pacific,* 3) *Kiss Me, Kate,* 4) *The King and I,* and 5) *The Mystery of Edwin Drood.*

256A. Flaemmchen in the 1989 musical *Grand Hotel* established in dialogue (at least during the Boston tryout) that her name translates to "The Flame," which is the name of a Kander and Ebb song from their first Broadway show *Flora the Red Menace*.

257A. Each musical has a song that corresponds to a card in a playing deck.

1) "The Joker," 2) "It Takes Two," 3) "Three Sunny Rooms," 4) "Four Black Dragons," 5) "Five Growing Boys," 6) "Six Months out of Every Year," 7) "The Seven Deadly Virtues," 8) "Tonight at Eight," 9) "About a Quarter to Nine," 10) "Ten Little Indians," 11) "Bobby and Jackie and Jack," 12) "The Acid Queen," 13) "The King of New York," and 14) "Ace in the Hole."

258A. Sherman Edwards wrote the score to *1776*, which won the Tony for Best Musical in 1969.

It included among its characters Roger *Sherman*, the delegate from Connecticut, and *Edward* Rutledge, the delegate from South Carolina.

259A. *Musical Husbands*, the mythical musical that *Merrily We Roll Along*'s equally mythical Franklin Shepard and Charley Kringas wrote in 1964, was said by producer Joe Josephson (played by Jason Alexander, by the way) to be "*Funny Girl, Fiddler,* and *Dolly* combined."

Funny Girl ran 1,348 performances; *Fiddler* amassed 3,242; and *Dolly* made it to 2,844. Their grand total is 7,434 performances.

260A. Novelist T. H. White wrote *The Once and Future King*, which Alan Jay Lerner and Frederick Loewe turned into *Camelot* in 1960.

Three years later, historian Theodore H. White interviewed Jacqueline Kennedy after her husband's assassination. There she referenced President John F. Kennedy's affection for the musical; since then, his administration has become known as "Camelot."

261A. "Make the Most of Your Music," which Sondheim wrote to replace "Live, Laugh, Love" in the 1987 London version of *Follies,* quotes Edvard Grieg's "Piano Concerto in A Minor."

It became "Hill of Dreams" in *Song of Norway.*

Its melody is also heard in "Rosemary" in *How to Succeed in Business Without Really Trying.*

262A. The label for "Day by Day" said that its singer was "Godspell"—the name of the musical, of course.

263A. These songs all mention people who don't appear in the musical.

1) Elsie, 2) Mrs. Mooney, 3) Leon, 4) Lipschitz and Strauss, 5) Marigold Coneybear, and 6) Angel's boyfriends Sam, Fred, Joey, (and possibly Pete).

264A. The job is President of the United States.

George M. Cohan played Franklin Delano Roosevelt in *I'd Rather Be Right.*

Len Cariou portrayed Theodore Roosevelt in *Teddy & Alice.*

Dee Hoty played Miss Mona Stangley, who was elected to the office in *The Best Little Whorehouse Goes Public.*

(Yes, in the 1994 sequel to *The Best Little Whorehouse in Texas,* the former madam of the Chicken Ranch is elected President of the United States. That should tell you why the show ran sixteen performances.)

265A. Before *Sweet Charity* began its pre-Broadway tryout, Barbra Streisand recorded its song "You Wanna Bet?"

But Dorothy Fields eventually wrote new lyrics to create "Sweet Charity."

Although her new words were kept verbatim in the film, Cy Coleman wrote a new melody for them.

266A. In *West Side Story*, Tony, when speaking about Maria to Doc, says that the way he feels is like taking "a trip to the moon" where "it isn't a man that's up there, Doc. It's a girl, a lady."

267A. The key word is "play," for that's what the 1958 Broadway attraction *Say, Darling* was about, the creation of the mythical musical *The Girl from Indiana*.

Styne, Comden, and Green wrote songs that this musical supposedly had. Each actress who came to audition had chosen to sing the then-very-popular "I Could Have Danced All Night" from Lerner and Loewe's *My Fair Lady*.

268A. Judy Holliday's picture on the window card for her 1963 musical *Hot Spot* was actually one from her Tony-winning performance in *Bells Are Ringing*.

(Budgetary problems, we presume?)

269A. As detailed in his biomusical *A Class Act*, Edward Kleban was a record producer by day and an aspiring writer of Broadway musicals by night.

For the former, he was Grammy-nominated for producing the original cast album of *Hallelujah, Baby!* For the latter, he won a Tony as the lyricist of *A Chorus Line*.

270A. *Good* (C. P. Taylor's only Broadway effort) played the Booth Theatre, which is situated next to what was then the Plymouth Theatre, where *Plenty* (David Hare's first Broadway drama) played.

Those two titles might bring to mind a certain licorice treat.

271A. Frank Loesser, between *Guys and Dolls* and *How to Succeed in Business Without Really Trying*, wrote *The Most Happy Fella*.

In it, the aging Tony Esposito pursues the much younger Amy. It opened on May 3, 1956, and closed on December 14, 1957.

272A. George S. Kaufman chose Howard Teichmann as his collaborator on *The Solid Gold Cadillac,* which opened on Broadway in 1953 with Josephine Hull in the lead.

For the 1956 film, Judy Holliday succeeded her.

273A. The actual titles of those songs are "Shoeless *Joe* from Hannibal, Mo" and "Soon It's Gonna *Rain*"—but according to Steve, a miner in *Paint Your Wagon,* "The rain is Tess; the fire's Joe."

274A. *Rigadoon* was the working title for Lerner and Loewe's 1947 musical *Brigadoon.*

275A. Dolly asks Irene Molly, "Who took the horses out of Jenny Lind's carriage and pulled her through the streets?"

Michael Stewart's 1980 musical *Barnum* had Jenny Lind as a character.

276A. The title song of *Do I Hear a Waltz?*—lyrics by Stephen Sondheim, music by Richard Rodgers—has the phrase "such lovely Blue Danube-y music!" which refers to Johan Strauss II's "The Blue Danube" Waltz.

277A. Each of those musicals had a live animal in their original Broadway productions.

1) a mouse, 2) a lamb, 3) a seal), 4) a horse, 5) a dog, and 6) a goat.

278A. *A Little Night Music,* which won the prize in the 1972–1973 season, and *Nine,* which turned the trick in the 1981–1982 semester, both start their overtures with performers vocalizing rather than with musicians playing selections from the score.

279A. Each song mentions one of New York City's five boroughs.

1) Manhattan, 2) Brooklyn, 3) the Bronx, 4) Queens, and 5) Staten Island.

280A. "Starting here, starting now, everything's coming up roses," Rose sings in *Gypsy*.

Richard Maltby Jr. and David Shire wrote a song "Starting Here, Starting Now," which Barbra Streisand recorded on her 1966 album *Color Me Barbra*.

A decade later, *Starting Here, Starting Now* became the title of a revue of Maltby-Shire songs.

281A. *New Faces of 1952, New Faces of 1956, New Faces of 1962,* and *New Faces of 1968* all began with a song that songwriter Ronny Graham literally called "Opening" (aka "You've Never Seen Us Before").

282A. Maureen Stapleton played in all three one-act plays of *Plaza Suite* in 1968.

In the 1971 film version, she was relegated to the first play while Barbara Harris succeeded her in the second, and Lee Grant in the third.

283A. Each of them includes a made-up word.

1) Rockerfellative, 2) Shuberty, 3) Beelzebubble, 4) Rhodadandy, 5) Walkerman, 6) Sondheimlich, 7) Rejoicify, and 8) Daddily.

284A. Jerry Herman and Harvey Fierstein's *La Cage aux Folles* bested Sondheim's *Sunday in the Park with George* for Best Musical in 1983–1984.

In the 2004–2005 race, it emerged triumphant over *Pacific Overtures* as Best Musical Revival.

Then, in 2010–2011, it conquered *A Little Night Music* as Best Musical Revival.

285A. Arnold Ziffel, the pig in the semi-beloved TV series, had a cameo in *1776*. Look for him in the scene where Adams and Franklin walk to Jefferson's room to see how he's progressing with the Declaration of Independence.

286A. "Nowadays" from *Chicago,* says, "In fifty years or so, it's gonna change, you know." Indeed it did for Sondheim's *Company,* which, fifty years or so later, certainly changed when its leading character went from a man named Bobby to a woman named Bobbie.

287A. Jerry Herman, who wrote the scores for *Milk and Honey* and *Hello, Dolly!* had in the musicals a widow who wanted to remarry but felt the need to ask her deceased husband for permission.

Clara in the first show sings "A Hymn to Hymie." Dolly in the second has her "Ephraim, let me go" speech.

288A. These musicals have songs that list the colors of the spectrum, commonly made into the acronym R O Y G B I V.

1) "Red Ryder Carbine Action BB Gun," 2) "Orange Girl," 3) "Yellow Shoes," 4) "Green Finch and Linnet Bird," 5) "Blue Wind," 6) "Mood Indigo," and 7) "Violets and Silverbells."

289A. Leslie Bricusse wrote the score to *Say Hello to Harvey,* the musical version of *Harvey,* which closed in 1981 in Toronto without braving Broadway.

290A. Irving Berlin's 1918 musical was called *Yip-Yip-Yaphank,* produced thirty-two years before *Call Me Madam,* which would win a Tony for Best Score.

E. Y. Harburg, lyricist of *Finian's Rainbow* and many other musicals, sported the nickname Yip.

291A. They all have the word "Avenue" in their titles. 1) *Avenue Q,* 2) *Avenue X,* and 3) "Avenue A" from the TV musical *Mrs. Santa Claus.*

292A. Bennett's first impulse was to have director-choreographer Zach reject Cassie. Marsha Mason (then the wife of Neil Simon, who had doctored the script) urged Bennett to have Zach give Cassie the job.

Had he not chosen her, Tony-winner Donna McKechnie's character would have experienced the same fate as Sheila (Tony-winner Kelly Bishop) and Paul (Tony-winner Sammy Williams), neither of whom would appear in Zach's musical.

293A. "L'il" is the contraction. Mercer's 1949 musical was called *Texas, L'il Darlin'*. His 1956 hit that became a film was *L'il Abner*.

294A. In 2020, John Bolton, best known as the United States' twenty-sixth National Security Advisor, wrote a book called *The Room Where It Happened*—quoting a song from *Hamilton*.

But John Bolton is also a Broadway performer who played "The Old Man" in the 2012 musical *A Christmas Story*, in which he wins a contest and receives a lamp in the shape of a leg, which he is told (and believes) is "a major award."

295A. It would have been apt if McKinley Belcher III, on his way to audition for Happy in the 2022 revival of *Death of a Salesman*, sang to himself a song from the 1925 musical *No, No, Nanette*: "I Want to Be Happy."

296A. Casey Nicholaw was a performer in each, be it in the ensemble or in small roles. As of this writing, he's a Tony-winning director and six-time Tony-nominee for Best Choreography.

(Shall we all sing a chorus of "It's Not Where You Start, It's Where You Finish?" from *Seesaw*?)

297A. *South Pacific*, which ran 1,925 performances—287 fewer than then-champion *Oklahoma!*—closed on January 16, 1954.

That was precisely ten years to the day before *Hello, Dolly!* opened on January 16, 1964. It would eventually eclipse those two Rodgers and Hammerstein hits and *My Fair Lady*, too, as Broadway's longest-running musical.

298A. The musicals were *Nick & Nora* and *Song & Dance*.

For the former, Richard Maltby Jr. received a nomination for his lyrics; for the latter, he received three, as director, lyricist, and coproducer.

299A. "Maine" comes from *No Strings*, which won the 1961–1962 Tony for Best Score.

The state was admitted to the union on March 15, 1820—142 years before the show officially opened on March 15, 1962.

300A. "Momma's Turn" from *Upstairs at O'Neal's* has mothers of then-critics Mel Gussow, Clive Barnes, Frank Rich, and John Simon discuss the musicals they'd seen.

301A. The title song of *Sherry!* was the nickname of Sheridan Whiteside, the centerpiece of the 1967 musical version of *The Man Who Came to Dinner.*

It is, however, not to be confused with the Four Seasons's 1962 hit "Sherry," which was a highlight of the 2005 musical *Jersey Boys.*

302A. Henry Higgins in *My Fair Lady* was played by Rex Harrison, who won a Best Actor in Musical Tony in 1956–1957.

Harold Hill in *The Music Man* was portrayed by 1957–1958 Tony-winner Robert Preston.

Higgins asked "Why can't a woman be more like a man?" while Hill insisted on "The Sadder-but-Wiser Girl for Me."

303A. When John Travolta, Jeff Conaway, Olivia Newton-John, and Stockard Channing were playing seniors at Rydell High School in *Grease,* they were respectively 23, 27, 29, and 33 years old.

(Thus, Channing was almost twice the age of the average high school senior.)

304A. In *Bye Bye Birdie,* neither the engaged Rosie and Albert nor puppy-lovers Hugo and Kim say "I love you."

Kim's father, Mr. McAfee, is the character who says it—not to any-one in his family, but to Ed Sullivan in "Hymn for a Sunday Evening."

305A. *Assassins* always had a scene set on November 22, 1963, where a few historical assassins helped persuade Lee Harvey Oswald to shoot President John F. Kennedy.

Later in the musical's genesis, however, Stephen Sondheim decided to add "Something Just Broke," a song in which various Americans recalled where they were and what they were doing when they heard the news.

306A. "Me and My Shadow" from the 1986 musical *Big Deal* was also sung by Judy Garland at the Palace in 1967.

And wouldn't at least the title "Me and My Shadow" be apt for Mary Martin's first song in *Peter Pan*?

307A. "The Diary of Adam and Eve" was the first section of the three-act musical *The Apple Tree*.

So if we wanted to aggrandize and exaggerate the "scandal" of Coo-persmith's quitting/firing, we could use the name of the character for which Ray Walston received his Tony for *Damn Yankees*—Applegate.

308A. *Ballroom* starred Dorothy Loudon, who'd won a Tony for *Annie,* and Vincent Gardenia, who'd scored one for *The Prisoner of Second Avenue.*

Both performers would receive nominations for *Ballroom,* too, but Lynn Roberts and Bernie Knee (as Marlene and Nathan, the band's singers) had more musical numbers than they did.

309A. In *West Side Story*, the Sharks, after being thrown out of Doc's Candy Shop by Lieutenant Shrank, sardonically whistle "America" to comment on how the country has failed them.

This is not the "America" that Stephen Sondheim and Leonard Bernstein wrote, but the patriotic song that begins "My country, 'tis of thee."

310A. "Kismet" is a Turkish word meaning "fate."

"Fate" is the third song in *Kismet,* the 1953–1954 Tony-winning Best Musical.

311A. In *70, Girls, 70,* Mr. and Mrs. McIllehenny in "You and I, Love" imagine they have the option of seeing a TV show that night on which Tiny Tim will appear.

No, this has nothing to do with *A Christmas Carol.* Tiny Tim was the stage name of Herbert Khaury, a falsetto-voiced, scraggly haired singer who enjoyed a brief vogue in the late 1960s.

312A. Because snippets of "Remember," "Soon," and "The Glamorous Life" are all sung in the so-called overture, one could stretch the definition of reprise to say that when they're fully sung later in act 1, that's exactly what they are.

313A. In 2014, Nathan Lane starred in Terrence McNally's *It's Only a Play,* ten years after he'd starred in (and had somewhat rewritten) *The Frogs.*

The score by Stephen Sondheim includes the song "It's Only a Play."

314A. "Gawk, Tousle and Shucks" is the official title of that song from *How Now, Dow Jones.*

315A. Bob Merrill. Just as Charles Strouse wrote the film score music to *Bonnie and Clyde,* and Frank Wildhorn wrote the music for the Broadway musical *Bonnie and Clyde,* Henry Mancini wrote the film score to *Breakfast at Tiffany's* and Bob Merrill wrote the music (and the lyrics, too) to the Broadway musical *Breakfast at Tiffany's.*

316A. Chita Rivera is the legend; Cheetah was a discotheque that *Hair* played between debuting at the Anspacher and moving to the Biltmore.

317A. Each of them has a character who has a description as part of his or her name.

1) Lucy the Slut, 2) Marco the Magnificent, 3) Harry the Horse, 4) Horton the Elephant, and 5) Karen the Computer.

318A. You might assume that it's Domina, given that she haughtily sings "Nothing that's Greek" just before Pseudolus adds, "She plays Medea later this week."

But according to Sondheim's published lyrics for "Comedy Tonight," it's "a tall, buxom young woman"—namely, Gymnasia.

319A. In 1966, Maria Irene Fornes wrote a play called *The Office* that started previews at the theater now known as The Sondheim. The play never opened, despite having Jerome Robbins as its director.

Almost forty years later, *The Office* became a popular TV series from 2005–2013; it was parodied as a musical at the Theatre Center in 2018.

320A. Carol Burnett yawns at the end of the original cast album of *Once Upon a Mattress,* in which Jack Gilford appeared. You can hear him yawn during "I'm Calm" on the original cast album of *A Funny Thing Happened on the Way to the Forum.*

321A. Mitch Leigh provided the music for the acclaimed *Man of La Mancha* in 1965 and the out-of-town closer *Chu Chem* in 1967 (although that one semi-rebounded with a failed Broadway production in 1989).

But in 1970, his musical of William Alfred's *Hogan's Goat* was called *Cry for Us All* when it had its world premiere in New Haven, then *Who to Love* when it opened in Boston, before returning to *Cry for Us All* for its nine-performance run at the Broadhurst.

322A. *Gypsy.* Ethel Merman, who played Rose, won a Tony for *Call Me Madam.*

Jack Klugman, who portrayed Herbie, won one Emmy for *The Defenders* and two for *The Odd Couple.*

The other man is Stephen Sondheim, who played Pop on the recording. He filled in for Erv Harmon on "Some People" by saying "You ain't gettin' 88 cents from me, Rose."

PART THREE

ANSWERS

I'M A GENIUS GENIUS

323A. Considering that Rodgers's 1976 musical *Rex* concerned Henry VIII's disposing of some of his wives, *Henry, Sweet Henry* (the title of Merrill's 1967 musical) wouldn't have been a good description of His Highness.

324A. Each song contained a topical reference that's no longer topical.

1) "Hollanderize" refers to the Joseph Hollander company that was the leader in dyeing furs.

2) "The Automat" refers to coin-operated machines that dispensed food in restaurants in New York City from 1912 to 1991.

3) The ballclub known as the Washington Senators had its first iteration from 1901–1960, before moving to Minnesota; a replacement Washington Senators played in the nation's capital from 1961 to 1971, and then moved to Texas.

4) Borders, a chain of bookstores, went out of business in 2011.

5) George Bush as president was indeed only for then.

6) "A nickel Coke" is certainly unattainable today.

325A. You'd only get the answer to this one if you remembered that the musical version of *The Full Monty* takes place in Buffalo—and that Bobby says in the Tony and Pulitzer Prize–winning *A Chorus Line,* "to commit suicide in Buffalo is redundant."

326A. The list in that order references Broadway's four longest-running nonmusicals.

1) *By Jupiter* has a song, "Life with Father," the longest-runner.

2) *On the Town* in "Come Up to My Place" mentions *Tobacco Road,* the second-longest runner.

3) "I'm Still Here" cites *Abie's Irish Rose,* the third longest-runner.

4) The fourth-longest runner is *Gemini. I Can Get It for You Wholesale* has a song called "When Gemini Meets Capricorn" (although, granted, Elliot Gould and Marilyn Cooper pronounce it as *Geminee,* as many did in the 1930s, the time in which the musical was set).

327A. Dorothy Heyward cowrote the play *Porgy,* on which *Porgy and Bess* is based. But in 1943, she cowrote a play called—yes—*South Pacific,* which only ran five performances.

Six years later, Rodgers and Hammerstein must have assumed that no one would remember it and thus felt free to use the title.

328A. In early 1967, only a few weeks after *Cabaret* had opened, its lyricist Fred Ebb saw his adaptation of Rodgers and Hart's 1942 hit *By Jupiter* open in an off-Broadway revival.

329A. Al Hirschfeld drew each of their logos.

330A. Vandergelder in "It Takes a Woman" asks, "To whom can you turn when the plumbing is leaking?"

Georgina in "My Own Morning" yearns for the day when there's "No one to whom I'm beholden."

Given each character's lack of education, Vandergelder would more likely state, "Who can you turn to when the plumbing is leaking?" Similarly speaking, Georgina would say "No one I'm beholden to."

331A. *The Music Man,* which won the 1957–1958 Best Musical Tony, hired a professional barbershop quartet known as the Buffalo Bills.

That's also the name of a New York football club.

(We never specified New York *City,* did we?)

332A. Those four names are also the names of legitimate theaters in London's West End.

333A. *A Chorus Line.* This fact was actually printed in the musical's first-edition *Playbill.* It also gave an alphabetical listing of the shows in question from *A Joyful Noise* to *Your Own Thing.*

(For those who believe that *A Joyful Noise* should be listed under J, recall that Michael Bennett, *A Chorus Line's* auteur, was inclined to call it *Chorus Line* until he realized that *A Chorus Line* would put it at the top of the list alphabetically in the *New York Times.*)

334A. The 1959 musical *Once Upon a Mattress* has a dance called "The Spanish Panic." That name was retained for the 1964 TV version, but for the 1972 TV version, the name of the dance was changed to "The Polish Panic."

335A. Each has an important character who uses a middle initial.

1) Melvin P. Thorpe, 2) Alfred P. Doolittle, 3) Frank N. Furter, 4) Squidward Q. Tentacles, and 5) Caldwell B. Caldwell.

336A. Byron Prong is the last-billed performer listed on the front-of-house display for *Midsummer Madness,* the play that starred Vera Charles in the 1958 film version of *Auntie Mame,* whose screenplay was written by Betty Comden and Adolph Green.

In 1964, when they wrote *Fade Out–Fade In,* they gave the same name to the character played by Jack Cassidy, who only months before had won a Best Featured Actor in a Musical Tony for playing Steven Kodaly in *She Loves Me.*

337A. An exclamation point followed the title of each musical.

1) *Oklahoma!,* 2) *Fiorello!,* 3) *Hello, Dolly!,* 4) *Heathen!,* 5) *Sarafina!,* and 6) *Play On!*

338A. Producer Harold S. Prince eventually became more commonly known as Hal Prince.

Reverse those names, and you'll get Prince Hal, who's called that quite often in Shakespeare's *Henry IV, Parts I and II.*

339A. Charlie Brown, Lucy, Linus, and Schroeder are all seen writing "a book report on *Peter Rabbit.*"

True, Lily Garland doesn't write a book report, but she does sign the name "Peter Rabbit" on her contract to thwart would-be-director Oscar Jaffee.

340A. The 1974 musical *Over Here!* had Pauline de Paul and Paulette de Paul (as the two surviving Andrews Sisters, Patty and Maxene), needing a third singer to make an effective trio.

They found one in Mitzi, who in reality was a Nazi spy. Eventually Mitzi was suspected as such, and she was challenged to prove that she was a loyal American by reciting the entire second stanza of "The Star-Spangled Banner," which she started.

But she got only as far as those three sentences, when the person accusing her had all the ammunition he needed: "No real American *knows* the second stanza of 'The Star-Spangled Banner!'"

341A. Michael J. Pollard was nominated as Best Supporting Actor in 1967 for *Bonnie and Clyde.*

A year later, Kay Medford was nominated as Best Supporting Actress for *Funny Girl.*

Although both had appeared in the original cast of *Bye Bye Birdie*—he as Hugo Peabody, she as Mae Peterson—neither he nor she had a song in it.

342A. Angela Lansbury won the Best Actress in a Musical Tony for portraying Mrs. Lovett in *Sweeney Todd* (which won the 1978–1979 Best Musical Tony, too).

Dorothy Loudon (a previous Best Actress in a Best Musical Tony-winner for *Annie*) was her replacement.

Lansbury (among others) sang "Nowhere to Go But Up" in *Mary Poppins Returns*. Indeed, *Nowhere to Go But Up* was Loudon's first Broadway show in 1962.

343A. In the 1964 musical *High Spirits,* Elvira, a ghost who's visited earth, now decides in her eleven o'clock number to return to "Home, Sweet Heaven," where her friends include Greek poet Homer.

A musical called *Home Sweet Homer* opened and closed on January 4, 1976.

344A. All were beauty contest winners in various pageants.

1) Miss Saigon (*Miss Saigon*), 2) Young American Miss (*Smile*), 3) Miss Baltimore Crabs (*Hairspray*), and 4) Miss Watermelon, Miss Southern Comfort, *and* Miss Cotton Blossom (*Subways Are for Sleeping*).

345A. The Spielberg movie is his 1979 film called *1941.*

Switch the two numbers in the middle and you get *1491,* a musical by Meredith (*The Music Man*) Willson about Columbus, which closed in California in 1969.

346A. Fernando Lamas was Ethel Merman's leading man—and adversary—in *Happy Hunting* in 1956. The apex of their feud occurred at a performance when, after they kissed, he dramatically wiped it off on his sleeve.

Lamas's son Lorenzo, mentioned in "Great Big Stuff" in *Dirty Rotten Scoundrels,* hotly defended his father to your author: "That just happened once!" he insisted.

347A. "A Gentleman's Gentleman" in *Darling of the Day* included E. Y. Harburg's command, "Don't be so uppity to the man who serves your cup of tea."

348A. Irene Sharaff was replaced by Alvin Colt as costume designer on *Guys and Dolls.* But she had the last laugh five years later when she was hired to do the film.

She had an even bigger laugh later still when she received her Oscar nomination for Best Costume Design in Color.

349A. Mary Martin's first starring role was in 1943, when she played Venus (a statue that came to life) during the 567-performance *One Touch of Venus.*

At one point Venus stood in front of a psychiatrist who asked her age. Venus replied that only Homer and Virgil could say for sure. When he asked where he could find them, Venus matter-of-factly said, "Go to hell." She wasn't using an epithet; she was specifying a location.

Martin's last starring role in a musical was in 1966, in the 560-performance *I Do! I Do!* where she played wife to a husband played by Robert Preston. The last line of their fight song, "The Honeymoon Is Over," has both of them proclaiming "Go to hell!"

Needless to say, it's not an expression that Martin would have said either as Postulant Maria or even Mrs. von Trapp in *The Sound of Music.*

350A. The musical in question is *Man of La Mancha;* the Aldonza in that revival was Mary Elizabeth Mastrantonio.

Roger De Bris shares her middle name, for his is Elizabeth as well.

351A. Each of the titles of their opening numbers is in another language.

1) "Chanson," 2) "Willkommen," 3) "Valse Milieu," 4) "Shalom," 5) "Dites-Moi," and 6) "Aquarius."

(Yes, "Aquarius" is, after all, a Latin word.)

352A. *Merrily We Roll Along*'s "Bobby and Jackie and Jack" doesn't stop there after it has named three members of the Kennedy family.

It will reference fourteen in all: Ethel, Teddy, Pat, Eunice, Peter, Jean, Joan, Stephen, Sargent, Joe, and Rose; some were to the manner born, while others married well.

353A. Lucy Van Pelt, already (in)famous because of the comic strip *Peanuts,* received additional visibility through the 1967 off-Broadway musical *You're a Good Man, Charlie Brown.*

After the song "Schroeder," in which she fails to interest the piano prodigy, she concedes "My Aunt Marion was right. Never try to discuss marriage with a musician."

354A. Ethel Merman's beau in *Anything Goes* in 1934 was Sir Evelyn Oakleigh.

Twelve years later, Merman would play Annie Oakley in *Annie Get Your Gun.*

355A. Each of those songs served as the title of a book written by one of the song's creators.

1) Stephen Sondheim, 2) Charles Strouse, 3) Mary Rodgers, and 4) Richard Adler.

356A. Maria's father in *West Side Story* interrupts the conversation she's having with Tony with his offstage "Maruca!"

357A. Cha-Cha Di Gregorio appears in act 2 of *Grease.*

"Mu-Cha-Cha" opens act 2 of *Bells Are Ringing.*

358A. The Garbo film is *Camille*.

In *Take Me Along*, which opened October 22, 1959, and ran fourteen months, Muriel fantasizes in "I Would Die" that she'd "gotten what Camille had."

In *The Sound of Music*, which opened November 16, 1959 (and in a way has been running ever since), Elsa Schraeder tells Captain von Trapp in "How Can Love Survive?" that "I cannot die like Camille for you."

359A. Even though "Love in Bloom" does *not* open the original cast album of *Two Gentlemen of Verona*, the musical indeed did open with it.

A character named Thurio sang what had been nominated as Best Original Song in 1934 (the first time that award was given) in a film called *She Loves Me Not*.

360A. Bernadette Peters won a 1985–1986 Tony for *Song & Dance*. She did a one-woman show in act 1 (*Song*); then dancers took over for *Dance*.

At one point during that second act, she walked across from stage left to stage right, exited, and wasn't seen again until the curtain calls.

361A. Shakespeare created the expressions that provided a song title for each of the musicals.

1) "Love Is Blind," 2) "Knock, Knock," 3) "Forever and a Day," and 4) "Wild Goose Chase."

362A. In the autumn of 1963, when *Hello, Dolly!* was in Detroit, producer David Merrick decided that composer-lyricist Jerry Herman needed help, and summoned Bob Merrill, Charles Strouse, and Lee Adams to buttress the score.

(How much the three did or didn't do will probably never be known for sure.)

After *Hello, Dolly!* opened to raves, Herman was the Tony-winning toast of Broadway. So he was summoned in the autumn of 1964 to contribute songs for *Ben Franklin in Paris.* He wrote "Too Charming" and "To Be Alone with You."

363A. The musical is *Fiorello!* "Little Tin Box" mentions a Rolls-Royce. In the very next song—"The Very Next Man"—a Chevrolet is cited.

364A. The Tony-nominated composer-lyricist is James Taylor, who received the honor for writing the music and lyrics for two songs—and the music for one—in *Working.*

From 1972 to 1983, he was married to Carly Simon, who's mentioned in *The Full Monty*'s "Big Ass Rock."

365A. Martin Charnin played Big Deal in the original cast of *West Side Story.* He participated in the comic number "Gee, Officer Krupke," in which one of Stephen Sondheim's lyrics was "leapin' lizards!"

It's an expression that was made famous by Little Orphan Annie. Eventually, Charnin would have the idea to musicalize and direct *Annie.*

366A. All five shows were confident enough that they'd come in that they actually had signage up at the Broadway theaters they'd booked.

1) Marquis, 2) Martin Beck, 3) St. James, 4) The Music Box, and 5) Marquis yet again.

367A. You might have noticed that many of the clues point to Barbra Streisand, but would such a megastar pony up for a cast album recording session?

According to Albert Poland, the musical's producer, she indeed did.

368A. Every full Leonard Bernstein score has at least one song that begins with or includes the letters *qu*.

1) "Times S*qu*are Ballet" (*On the Town*), 2) "A *Qu*iet Girl" (*Wonderful Town*), 3) "*Qu*iet" (*Candide*), 4) "*Qu*intet" (*West Side Story*), and 5) "On 10 S*qu*are Miles on the Potomac River" (*1600 Pennsylvania Avenue*).

369A. The 1962 play *Isle of Children* advertised that "Patty Duke Talks!"

For, aside from "wah-wah" at the end of *The Miracle Worker* (for which she didn't receive a Tony nomination, but did eventually win an Oscar), she didn't speak.

370A. The musical is the 1955 hit *Damn Yankees,* in which Ray Walston, playing Mr. Applegate (read: the Devil), uses those words to describe Lola.

She was played by Gwen Verdon, who in twenty years would be the leading lady of *Chicago.*

371A. Each of them has a song that also is the title of a Tony-winning musical.

1) "Once," 2) "Applause," 3) "Contact," 4) "Big River," and 5) "My Fair Lady."

372A. The 1964 revival of *Hamlet* had six performers who'd previously appeared in Broadway musicals: Richard Burton (Hamlet; *Camelot*), Alfred Drake (Claudius; *Kiss Me, Kate,* among others), Eileen Herlie (Gertrude; *Take Me Along* and *All American*), William Redfield (Mercury; *Out of This World,* among others), John Cullum (Laertes; *Camelot),* and even Philip Coolidge (Voltemand; *Kismet*).

Five would soon appear in at least one Broadway musical: George Rose (Gravedigger; *The Mystery of Edwin Drood,* among others); George Voskovec (Player King; a replacement Herr Schultz in

Cabaret), Barnard Hughes (Marcellus; *How Now, Dow Jones*), Robert Burr (Bernardo; *Bajour*), and even Gerome Ragni (Ensemble; *Hair*).

373A. Al Hirschfeld, who has a theater named for him on West 45th Street, was born on Kensington Avenue in St. Louis.

That's where "The Boy Next Door" lives in the 1944 film and 1989 Broadway musical *Meet Me in St. Louis,* which played the Gershwin Theatre.

374A. The first letters of 1) *Urinetown,* 2) *Nunsense,* 3) *Carrie,* 4) *Once,* 5) *Urban Cowboy,* 6) *Parade,* 7) *Lestat,* 8) *Evita,* and 9) *Drood,* if separated by periods and put together, become "U.N.C.O.U.P.L.E.D." from *Starlight Express.*

375A. Before Bock and Harnick opted for *The Apple Tree* as the title of their 1966 musical, it was to be called *Come Back! Go Away! I Love You!*

That title isn't so far afield from the one used for the 1996 hit revue *I Love You! You're Perfect! Now Change!*

376A. They mention luminaries who are pictured on US currency, and in the order of the bills' value:

1) $1—George Washington, 2) $2—Thomas Jefferson, 3) $5—Abraham Lincoln, 4) $10—Alexander Hamilton, 5) $20—Andrew Jackson, 6) $50—Ulysses S. Grant, 7) $100—Benjamin Franklin, and 8) $500—William McKinley.

377A. Every one of those musicals received multiple nominations; these artists were the only ones from their shows that lost.

378A. *Applause,* the 1969–1970 Best Musical Tony-winner, included a song called "She's No Longer a Gypsy."

Indeed, Chita Rivera, who had been playing Anyanka, a Gypsy in the musical *Bajour,* saw the musical close on June 12, 1965.

379A. Each musical has a character whose name ends in *o*. They are all arranged alphabetically.

1) Adolpho, 2) Bernardo, 3) Cleo, 4) Dromio, 5) Emilio, 6) Fiyero, 7) Guido, 8) Harpo, 9) Ito, 10) Jo, 11) Kangaroo, 12) Leo, 13) Manjiro, 14) Nero, 15) Otto, 16) Petruchio, 17) Quasimodo, 18) Rizzo, 19) Sancho, 20) Thurio, 21) Ugo, 22) Vittorio, 23) Waldo, 24) Yamato, and 25) Zeppo.

Notice that the letter *X* is not represented here, because, at least as of this writing, no character in any musical has ever had a name that begins with *X* and ends with an *o*.

380A. Paul Ford was a cast member but didn't partake in song in the notorious 1958 musical *Whoop-Up*.

Not long after, he took over as Mayor Shinn in *The Music Man*, which he would also play in the 1962 film.

He didn't sing in those, but at least he can be heard speaking on the 1960 cast album of *A Thurber Carnival*.

381A. *Company*, the 1970–1971 Tony-winning musical, saw its lead Dean Jones leave soon after he'd recorded the album. Larry Kert replaced him, and the Tony committee preferred to recognize him rather than Jones.

When the musical moved to London, Kert and the original cast went with it; his voice was superimposed over Jones's tracks to make "the London cast album"; only his rendition of "Being Alive" is now included as a bonus track on the CD.

382A. "We Sail the Seas," the opening number from *Ben Franklin in Paris*, names them all.

383A. All reference Rodgers and Hammerstein in one way or another.

1) Rodgers and Hammerstein unashamedly cited themselves when having a theatergoer sing "My love for my husband grew thinner the first time I looked at Yul Brynner."

2) The song starts with "Rodgers and Hammerstein proclaim 'There Is Nothing Like a Dame.'"

3) A belly dancer says that to properly perform she does need "a fringe without a surrey."

4) Connie Wong reminisces about appearing in *The King and I.*

5) Producer Joe Josephson hums a few almost-accurate measures from "Some Enchanted Evening."

6) Diana sings about "Xanax and Paxil and Buspar" and some others before deciding that "These are a few of my favorite pills."

384A. Although Ella Logan was much acclaimed in 1947 for *Finian's Rainbow,* she never again appeared on Broadway.

In 1965, she was expected to open at the Broadhurst Theatre in *Kelly,* but she was written out of the show during the Boston tryout.

Don Francks, who had played Kelly in that flop, later appeared as Woody Mahoney in the 1968 film of *Finian's Rainbow.*

385A. "Behold El Capitan" from the 1896 musical *El Capitan* was heard for a measure or so in "How I Saved Roosevelt" in *Assassins.*

The musical opened at Playwrights Horizons in 1991 and finally reached Roundabout's Studio 54 Theatre in 2004.

386A. The name of one character in each musical is an atypical one for its gender.

The Day before Spring, a 1945 Lerner and Loewe flop, has a female character named Christopher.

Pipe Dream, a 1955 musical that was Rodgers and Hammerstein's final failure, has a male character named Hazel.

387A. Each had a role in a Broadway musical that had won an Oscar for the performer in an earlier film incarnation.

1) P. J. Benjamin: Charlie, *Charlie and Algernon*; Cliff Robertson, *Charly*.

2) Ashley Brown: Mary, *Mary Poppins*; Julie Andrews, *Mary Poppins*.

3) Gloria De Haven: Diane, *Seventh Heaven*; Janet Gaynor, *Seventh Heaven*.

4) Johnny Johnston: Johnny, *A Tree Grows in Brooklyn*; James Dunn, *A Tree Grows in Brooklyn*.

5) Maria Karnilova: Hortense, *Zorba*; Lila Kedrova, *Zorba the Greek*.

6) Christopher Plummer: Cyrano, *Cyrano*; Jose Ferrer, *Cyrano de Bergerac*.

7) Martin Short: Elliot, *The Goodbye Girl*; Richard Dreyfus, *The Goodbye Girl*.

8) Laurence Naismith: Mr. Morgan, *A Time for Singing*; Donald Crisp, *How Green Was My Valley*.

9) Laurence Naismith: Kris Kringle, *Here's Love*; Edmund Gwenn, *Miracle on 34th Street*.

388A. Rex Harrison and Stanley Holloway, who'd star in *My Fair Lady* in 1956, had appeared in the film version of George Bernard Shaw's *Major Barbara* in 1941.

It starred Wendy Hiller, who had played Eliza Doolittle in the 1938 film of Shaw's *Pygmalion,* which of course would inspire *My Fair Lady.*

389A. David Rabe's 1971–1972 Tony-winner *Sticks and Bones* criticized family values and the Vietnam War.

To parody the former, Rabe chose to name his family members Ozzie, Harriet, David, and Ricky—the names of the Nelson family from the popular sitcom *The Adventures of Ozzie and Harriet* that ran from 1952 to 1966.

After CBS bought *Sticks and Bones* for broadcast, its powers-that-be felt changing the names to Andy, Ginger, Daniel, and Buck would keep viewers from being terribly confused (and lawyers from writing letters).

390A. Maurice Evans was a distinguished actor who made eleven Broadway appearances in six of Shakespeare's plays as well as taking the starring role in the 1960 musical *Tenderloin*.

That doesn't mean he was above playing a comic warlock in twelve episodes of *Bewitched* in the 1970s.

But in 1955, Evans had produced Ira Levin's *No Time for Sergeants*. Levin, whose musical *Drat! the Cat!* could only last a week in 1965, soon after had a hit novel in *Rosemary's Baby*. In the 1968 film version, Evans played Rosemary's friend who was one of her husband's victims.

391A. "Love Makes the World Go Round" was in *Carnival;* "Love Makes the World Go" was in *No Strings*.

The 1961–1962 Tonys saw a Best Actress in a Musical tie with Anna Maria Alberghetti winning for the former musical and Diahann Carroll for the latter.

392A. Starbuck in *110 in the Shade* admits to Lizzie that he was born with the name Smith. However, he felt it was too mundane and decided that he had to change it.

Starbuck/Smith was played by Robert Horton, who took the job after the musical in which he was supposed to star—Richard Rodgers and Alan Jay Lerner's *I Picked a Daisy*, about extrasensory perception—didn't come to fruition.

Lerner then teamed up with Burton Lane to write a musical on that subject, which became *On a Clear Day You Can See Forever*.

393A. Within the lyrics of each song is the title of the musical.

394A. In 1979, audiences at *They're Playing Our Song* heard Johnny Mathis's recording of "I Still Believe in Love," supposedly by Vernon Gersch and Sonya Walsk (but actually by Marvin Hamlisch and Carole Bayer Sager), when it was played over the theater's sound system.

In 1958, Mathis included on his *Johnny's Greatest Hits* album "All the Time" from Jay Livingston and Ray Evans's *Oh Captain!*

395A. That "Just one more thing"—mentioned twice—was a hint that the series in question is *Columbo.* Those four seemingly innocuous words were an expression that the title character said quite often after making a suspect think that he was no longer suspected.

Peter Falk, who starred in Neil Simon's *The Prisoner of Second Avenue*, played the title role on the series.

The play that preceded the series was called *Prescription: Murder*, which closed in Boston in 1962. Thomas Mitchell (best known for portraying Scarlett O'Hara's father in the 1939 *Gone with the Wind*) was its Lieutenant Columbo.

396A. The actual theater where *Merrily We Roll Along* played in 1981 was then named the Alvin. It was one of the last shows to play there before it was renamed the Neil Simon in 1983.

397A. Charles Webb is the author of *The Graduate*, a 1963 novel that became a blockbuster movie in 1967 and a Broadway play in 2002.

Charles Webb is also the name of Emily's father in the Pulitzer Prize–winning *Our Town*.

398A. Henry and Phoebe Ephron wrote *Take Her, She's Mine,* about their daughter's misadventures once she left home for college.

The young woman was Nora Ephron, who long after her rebellious Wellesley College days received Best Original Screenplay Oscar nominations for her work on *Sleepless in Seattle, Silkwood.* and *When Harry Met Sally.*

For the Broadway play, the Ephrons named the character Mollie. She was portrayed by Elizabeth Ashley, who won a Tony as Best Featured Actress in a Play.

399A. Both of those songs have triple rhymes of words that aren't remotely spelled the same.

"Magic to Do" has "study," "bloody," and "everybody."

"Necessity" has "tennis," "Venice," and "menace."

400A. *Jamaica* starred Lena Horne, albeit not at the Lena Horne Theatre but at the Imperial.

Its song "Incompatibility" defined that situation as "the classic disaster; look at Othello and Anna Lucasta."

401A. On both albums, a song proclaims, "Everything is rosy since I found my Rosie."

Although *R-o-s-i-e* is spelled differently from *r-o-s-y*, they still sound the same and therefore constitute an identity.

As for the soundtrack (and you do know, don't you, that "soundtrack" only refers to an album from a film or TV show and *not* a stage one?), the identity comes in "A Lot of Livin' to Do" where Kim sings "Handsome men from Yale or Purdue." *Do* and Pur*due* are identities.

402A. Lisa Mordente opened *Platinum* at the Mark Hellinger Theatre in 1978.

Not until 1983 did her mother—Chita Rivera—play there, courtesy of *Merlin*.

403A. Ethel Merman, who originated the title role in *Annie Get Your Gun*, did not receive a Tony because she and the 1946 musical predated the awards by a season.

But the *next* season, the Tonys began. By then, Mary Martin had taken the national company of *Annie Get Your Gun* on the road; she was awarded a Special Tony for doing just that.

404A. Shirley Booth, a 1952 Best Actress Oscar-winner for *Come Back, Little Sheba,* was directed by Jose Ferrer, a 1950 Best Actor Oscar-winner for *Cyrano De Bergerac,* in the 1959 musical *Juno.*

405A. You might not expect that a Japanese woman who was born in Otaru, Hokkaido, would be singing a Spanish-language song, but Miyoshi Umeki indeed recorded "Vaya Con Dios" before she performed in *Flower Drum Song* on both stage and screen.

406A. Jerry Herman would eventually write the scores for the Tony-winning Best Musicals *Hello, Dolly!* and *La Cage Aux Folles.*

Before those, in 1961 he wrote the score for *Milk and Honey.* It included "Hymn to Hymie," in which a widow lamented that since her husband passed away, she now buys only one lamb chop for her dinner, so the grocer gives her "a sympathetic look as he pastes a single stamp into my green stamp book."

The team of composer Charles Strouse and lyricist Lee Adams would also have two Best Musical Tony-winners: *Bye Bye Birdie* and *Applause.*

In between those, they provided the score for *"It's a Bird . . . It's a Plane . . . It's Superman."* Their song "What I've Always Wanted" had Lois Lane wistfully yearn for marriage and "green stamps in a book."

407A. In *Legs Diamond,* Peter Allen sang in "When I Get My Name in Lights" that he wants his "faci on the front page."

In *The Boy from Oz* (the biomusical about Peter Allen), Mitchel David Federan, playing the singer-composer-lyricist as a boy, sang that he wants to get his "picture on the front page."

"Faci" translates to "face," not "picture." But "face" has only one syllable, doesn't it?

408A. Charity, in "Where Am I Going," says she questions her options to "run to the Bronx, or Washington Square." The latter is the name of the Henry James 1880 novel, which in 1947 was also the name of the play that ran three days in New Haven and six in Boston before closing.

However, the husband-and-wife team of Ruth and Augustus Goetz who wrote it wouldn't give up on it. They rewrote and saw it open on Broadway a mere eight months later as *The Heiress*, where it ran almost a year. It has since had many Broadway revivals.

Olivia de Havilland won the 1949 Best Actress Oscar for playing the title role.

409A. When Jane Austen was writing the novel we now know as *Pride and Prejudice*, her working title was *First Impressions*.

Indeed, that was the title of the 1959 musical that had a book by Abe Burrows, the future Pulitzer Prize–winner for *How to Succeed in Business Without Really Trying*.

410A. Those seven musicals each had a backstage worker who won the Tony Award for Best Stage Technician. The prize was given from 1949 until 1963, after which it was retired.

411A. *Camelot* saw Richard Burton win the 1960–1961 Best Actor in a Musical Tony; Moss Hart wasn't nominated as its director.

Five or so years earlier, Burton had performed Hart's screenplay for *Prince of Players*, about Edwin and John Wilkes Booth. Burton portrayed Edwin and did scenes from *Hamlet*. He'd play that title role in his next Broadway assignment in 1964.

412A. Peter Allen's 1979 show *Up in One* gave a voice-over credit to Vernon Gersch.

Those who know *They're Playing Our Song* are aware that Vernon Gersch was the name of the character Robert Klein originated and was then playing in the 1979 hit musical.

To mask his identity as the voice-over artist, Klein chose to use his character's name and not his own.

413A. Granted, on the original cast album of *The Producers,* Mel Brooks sings only one couplet—"Don't be stupid! Be a smarty! Come and join the Nazi party!"

Still, he, an Oscar-winner for the screenplay of the first film of *The Producers,* qualifies.

(In fact, he repeated the line he had performed in the original 1968 film.)

414A. Harold Prince, who coproduced *The Pajama Game,* took over the direction of *A Family Affair.* It starred Shelley Berman, a stand-up comedian who made his fortune and reputation pretending to have trouble on the telephone when dealing with bureaucrats and incompetents.

In "Revenge," a song tailor-made for him, he had a harder time still when trying to cope with an answering machine in lieu of a genuine person.

415A. In the opening song of the 1951 revue *Two on the Aisle,* Betty Comden and Adolph Green condensed the plots of *Guys and Dolls, The King and I, Gentlemen Prefer Blondes,* and *Call Me Madam* into three-line summaries.

In "If," a woman groused that her beau hadn't taken her to *South Pacif* (shortened, of course, to rhyme with "if"). And in yet another song, "Catch Our Act at the Met," the character Aida in the opera of the same name is mentioned.

(And you were thinking of the Disney musical, weren't you?)

416A. In 1965, a year before Jerome Lawrence and Robert E. Lee had a 1,508-performance hit with *Mame,* they wrote a play called *Diamond Orchid,* about Paulita, a South American film actress who became the wife of a military man who would come to run the country where she would be its first lady.

Sounds like *Evita,* doesn't it?

Diamond Orchid ran five performances, less than 1/300th the run of *Evita*, which ran 1,567 performances.

417A. The famous person is Stephen Sondheim, whose father's name was Herbert.

Back in 1967, a show called *You Know I Can't Hear You When the Water's Running* was a collection of four one-act plays, one of which was called *I'm Herbert*.

Martin Balsam won a Tony for appearing in three of the plays, but he wasn't in *I'm Herbert*. So *that's* how a leading man could win a Tony for starring in a show without being in the play.

418A. Ruth Sherwood would have corrected some grammar: 1) "That's Him" to "That's He," 2) "Who to Love" to "Whom to Love," 3) "One Less Bell to Answer" to "One Fewer Bell to Answer," 4) "Me and Bobby McGee" to "Bobby McGee and I," and 5) "I Ain't Down Yet" to "I'm Not Down Yet."

419A. As of this writing the following have never seen a Tony-winning musical open in their theaters: 1) Ambassador, 2) American Airlines, 3) Belasco, 4) Booth, 5) Hayes, 6) Hudson, 7) James Earl Jones, 8) Lena Horne, 9) Lyric, 10) Samuel J. Friedman, 11) Stephen Sondheim, and 12) Studio 54.

420A. In 1948, four black-and-white film versions of Broadway musicals were released.

Are You with It, which had been a moderately successful 1945 musical, opened in March.

Up in Central Park, which had been a very successful 1945 musical, opened in July.

August brought the filmed version of the 1943 Broadway musical smash *One Touch of Venus*.

But finally in December, *Mexican Hayride* was released—without its songs, true, but it nevertheless was a film of a Broadway musical.

That's our answer.

421A. Eddie Conrad, a vaudevillian who appeared in those shows, had a wife named Birdie.

Yes, she was Birdie Conrad, which must have been the way that Conrad Birdie heard his name once he was in the army and endured roll calls.

422A. The musical is the 1966 hit *I Do! I Do!* It was produced by David Merrick, who had *Hot September* close in Boston a year earlier.

Its director-choreographer was Gower Champion, who'd have *Prettybelle* close in Boston five years later.

Bookwriter-lyricist Tom Jones and composer Harvey Schmidt wrote *Colette,* which closed in Denver in 1982.

The entire cast of *I Do! I Do!* consisted of "only" Mary Martin and Robert Preston. Martin had already experienced two musicals that had closed on the road: *Nice Goin'* in 1939 and *Dancing in the Streets* in 1943.

Robert Preston had endured *We Take the Town*'s shuttering in Philadelphia in 1962. A dozen years later, he would close *The Prince of Grand Street* in Boston.

423A. All of those songs mention automobiles.

1) Packard, 2) Gremlin, 3) Ferrari, 4) Mercedes-Benz, 5) Rolls-Royce, 6) Cadillac, 7) Chevrolet, 8) Pierce-Arrow, 9) Edsel and Volkswagen.

424A. *The Subject Was Roses* was the one and only show to play the Winthrop Ames Theatre at 240 West 44th Street.

That was the name of the playhouse from September 7, 1964, through March 21, 1965. It had been the Little Theatre from 1959 to 1964, and returned to that name in 1965, after *The Subject Was Roses* had closed.

In 1983, it became the Helen Hayes Theatre, after a different Helen Hayes Theatre on West 46th Street had been razed the year before.

Today it's known as the Hayes Theatre when its owner Second Stage has a production there and the *Helen* Hayes when the company rents it.

425A. *Promises, Promises*—the last musical to open on Broadway in the 1960s—had a repeated word in its title.

When Stephen Schwartz was a college student, he called the musical that he wrote *Pippin Pippin*.

426A. In 1975, Angela Lansbury won the Tony as Best Actress in a Musical for *Gypsy* while Rita Moreno won as Best Featured Actress for *The Ritz*.

Both ended their shows' first act by singing "Everything's Coming up Roses."

427A. George Spelvin, even though there *is* no George Spelvin. It's the fictitious name to which actors default when they don't want to be identified.

428A. If another *Carousel* character, Carrie Pipperidge Snow, had done the same, she'd have been C. P. Snow. His 1960 novel *The Affair* became a play later that year.

429A. The 1957 film *Twelve Angry Men* eventually wended its way to Broadway in 2004.

The film only named its characters Juror #1, Juror #2, and so on, and they were respectively played by 1) Martin Balsam, 2) John Fiedler, 3) Lee J. Cobb, 4) E. G. Marshall, 5) Jack Klugman, 6) Edward Binns, 7) Jack Warden, 8) Henry Fonda, 9) Joseph Sweeney, 10) Ed Begley, 11) George Voskovec, and 12) Robert Webber.

430A. The 1964 musical *Café Crown* starred Theodore Bikel who sang "Edelweiss" in *The Sound of Music*.

The 1965 musical *Drat! the Cat!* starred Barbra Streisand's then-husband Elliot Gould.

The third musical is *Man of La Mancha*, a 2,328 performance Best Musical Tony-winner.

The actor who appeared in all three was named Leo Bloom. Need I tell you in what film and Best Musical Tony-winner that character appears?

431A. Herb Gardner, whose *I'm Not Rappaport* won the 1985–1986 Best Play Tony, had two decades earlier designed the logo for *Flora the Red Menace*.

It showed a female picketer holding a sign that said "I Am" to the left of the words *Flora the Red Menace*. The print was tiny on that sign, but people would be well within their rights to assume that the musical was actually called *I Am Flora the Red Menace*.

432A. It played for four-and-a quarter years at two different theaters, from March 27, 1978, to June 27, 1982. It amassed 1,774 performances—enough to make it the twelfth longest-running musical in Broadway history.

But Bob Fosse's *Dancin'* couldn't land a recording contract.

Before you rebut, "But it was a dance show," remember that *Fosse* was, too—and yet RCA Victor recorded it soon after its 1999 debut.

433A. Jerry Herman's 1960 effort *Parade* has a song called "A Jolly Theatrical Season" in which two theater critics trade snarky remarks on the recent productions they'd seen.

434A. All had been previously adapted into musicals long before these later musicals ever came to pass.

Anastasia, produced in 2017, came well after Wright & Forrest's *Anya* in 1965.

Seventeen, a 1951 musical based on Booth Tarkington's novel, had been previously musicalized as *Hello, Lola* in 1926.

Some Like It Hot arrived on Broadway in 2022—fifty years after *Sugar*, the first iteration of the famous 1959 classic.

Let It Ride!, which debuted in 1961, arrived twenty years after *Banjo Eyes* in 1941.

Oh, Brother!, mounted in 1981, followed Rodgers and Hart's *The Boys From Syracuse* in 1938.

435A. When Tony winners Peter Stone, John Kander, and Fred Ebb were writing *Curtains* in the 1980s, it was to be set in that decade.

After Stone died and Rupert Holmes was approached to succeed him, he suggested setting the musical in 1959, which was an era before Frank Rich and almost before Sondheim.

436A. *Ain't Broadway Grand,* which played the Lunt-Fontanne in 1993, had music by Mitch *Leigh* of *Man of La Mancha* fame and lyrics by *Lee* Adams, who had won for *Bye Bye Birdie*.

437A. Mary Martin, whose *Jennie* opened and closed in 1963 after eighty performances, and Cyril Ritchard, whose *The Happiest Girl in the World* debuted and died after ninety-six performances in 1961, both starred in *Peter Pan* in 1954 and won Tonys.

She was born on December 1, 1913, sixteen years after he had come into the world on December 1, 1897.

438A. If you take the first letter of each title, they spell out "Sheila," which is (among other things) the name of the yacht in Sondheim and Perkins's 1973 film *The Last of Sheila*.

439A. *Carrie,* in which Betty Buckley played a mother who many would judge as mad, opened on May 12, 1988.

440A. The performers are Michael Rennie, Claude Rains, Fay Wray, Anne Francis, and Leo G. Carroll—all mentioned in "Science Fiction Double Feature" in *The Rocky Horror Show.*

441A. On August 27, 1978, a revival of Moss Hart and George S. Kaufman's *Once in a Lifetime* closed at Circle in the Square.

Uptown at what was then the State Theatre in Lincoln Center, a revival of *Stop the World, I Want to Get Off*—with a song called "Once in a Lifetime"—closed, too.

442A. All had two Tony nominees in the Best Actor in a Musical category.

1) Robert Goulet and David Wayne, 2) George Rose and Ian Richardson, 3) Kevin Kline and George Rose, 4) James Naughton and Gregg Edelman, 5) Brian Stokes Mitchell and Peter Friedman, 6) Norbert Leo Butz and George Lithgow, 7) Billy Porter and Stark Sands.

443A. Phil Silvers was offered Pseudolus in *A Funny Thing Happened on the Way to the Forum,* but refused.

Zero Mostel said yes, and won a Best Actor in a Musical Tony before repeating his role in the film, in which Silvers portrayed procurer Marcus Lycus.

However, in 1972, Silvers played Pseudolus in the musical's first Broadway revival and won the Best Actor in a Musical Tony that he might well have won nine years earlier.

444A. *Company,* which had a twenty-month run from April 1970 to January 1972, included "You Could Drive a Person Crazy," which Sondheim stated that he wrote in the style of the trio.

Then for eleven months, from February 1974 to January 1975, the two surviving Andrews Sisters—Patty and Maxene—sang new songs in their old style in *Over Here!* (and a postshow medley of old hits).

Finally, Bette Midler in her *Clams on the Half Shell Revue* sang the Andrews Sisters' vintage hit "Boogie Woogie Bugle Boy" for two months, from April 1975 to June 1975.

445A. In 1947, George Bernard Shaw's *Man and Superman* enjoyed a revival at the Alvin Theatre—nineteen years before the musical *"It's a Bird . . . It's a Plane . . . It's Superman"* debuted there.

446A. All of them don't end with the traditional musical theater "button," but instead fade out in the manner of a number of pop songs.

447A. Hattie Walker sings in "Broadway Baby" that "Hell, I'd even play the maid to be in a show."

And Maid was precisely the role that Dunaway accepted and played in *The Changeling*.

448A. The order represents, as of this writing, the number of Broadway revivals that each musical has had.

The Prom (none), *Evita* (one), *The Pajama Game* (two), *Hair* (three), *Gypsy* (four), *Peter Pan* (five), and *The Chocolate Soldier* (six).

449A. The musical is the 1957 Lena Horne vehicle *Jamaica*.

"Yankee Dollar" mentions Washington, Jefferson, Jackson, and Lincoln.

"Napoleon" cites Coolidge and Hoover.

"Push De Button" mentions Truman and Ike—the nickname for Eisenhower.

450A. The first time they won—respectively for *The Rose Tattoo, How to Succeed in Business Without Really Trying, The Music Man,* and *Pal Joey*—the Tonys were giving simple medallions as their awards.

The second time they won—respectively for *The Gingerbread Lady, Tru, I Do! I Do!,* and *No, No, Nanette*—the Tonys had been upgraded to statuettes.

451A. Each of these musicals has a song that mentions a sports team.

1) Boston Red Sox and Boston Braves: "Boston Beguine," 2) Cleveland Indians: "The Best of What This Country's Got," 3) New York Mets: "Come Back to Me," 4) Utah Jazz: "Turn It Off," and 5) Pittsburgh Steelers: "One Day."

452A. Although he's almost always called Hinesy in the 1954–1955 Best Musical Tony-winning *The Pajama Game,* his girlfriend Gladys lets us know that his actual name is Vernon.

The following year, Vernon was a Washington Senator in *Damn Yankees,* which later won the 1955–1956 Best Musical Tony.

453A. *Annie* opened on April 21, 1977—precisely forty-seven years after *Little Orchid Annie* debuted. The former ran 2,377 performances; the latter, a mere sixteen.

454A. *A Chorus Line* began its run at the Shubert on July 25, 1975, with music by Marvin Hamlisch.

Almost twenty years earlier, *The Wooden Dish* opened on October 15, 1955, at the Booth, which sits next to the Shubert. The musician who accompanied its twelve performances was Max Hamlisch.

455A. Although a name of a month was included in each title of each show, the show itself didn't open during that month.

January 17, 2008, marked the opening of *November.*

August 16, 1917, saw the debut of *Maytime.*

The Night of January 16 opened on the night of September 16, 1935.

456A. Their film versions used different titles.

1) *Gaslight,* 2) *Carnage,* 3) *Buffalo Bill and the Indians,* 4) *About Last Night,* and 5) *Summertime.*

457A. The musical that opened in May 1964, was *Fade Out–Fade In,* which was indeed doing capacity business until Carol Burnett fell ill enough to close the show.

One of its songs was "The Fiddler and the Fighter." In September 1964, *Fiddler on the Roof* indeed sported a fiddler, and in October 1964, *Golden Boy*'s main character was a fighter.

458A. *Everyday Rapture* had Betsy Wolfe and Lindsay Mendez as Sherie Rene Scott's backup singers.

Wolfe was later cast as Carrie in the 2018 revival of *Carousel* but ultimately didn't do it. She was replaced by Mendez, who then won a Tony as Best Supporting Actress in a Musical.

459A. In 1950, five years before she would star in Rodgers and Hammerstein's *Pipe Dream,* Helen Traubel, who had been much more comfortable in the opera world than Broadway, bought a piece of the St. Louis Browns.

By the time she took the stage of the Shubert, the team had already moved to become the Baltimore Orioles. A few years after, Traubel wrote her memoir, *St. Louis Woman.*

460A. All were born or have lived in their states' capital cities.

1) Phoenix, 2) Little Rock, 3) Atlanta, 4) Boston, and 5) Trenton.

461A. *The Sound of Music* (which opened on November 16, 1959) and *Fiorello!* (which debuted on November 23, 1959) are the two musicals.

Georg von Trapp and Fiorello LaGuardia, both of whom served in the military service and had fervent political beliefs, respectively died on May 30, 1947, and September 20, 1947.

462A. Natalie Wood, playing Maria in the first film version of *West Side Story*, sang "See that pretty girl in the mirror there!" in "I Feel Pretty."

Then, as Louise in the first film of *Gypsy*, before her appearance in "Wichita's one and only burlesque theater," she looked in the mirror and said "Momma . . . I'm pretty . . . I'm a pretty girl, Momma."

463A. *Once There Was a Russian* opened on February 18, 1961, and closed on, yes, February 18, 1961.

And yet, its one-performance run on Broadway was longer than the one achieved by its musical version *Pleasures and Palaces.*

Despite a book by Sam and Bella Spewack, the authors of *Kiss Me, Kate,* a score by Frank Loesser of *Guys and Dolls* and *How to Succeed in Business Without Really Trying* fame, and four-time Tony-winner Bob Fosse directing and choreographing, it closed in Detroit and thus ran no Broadway performances.

464A. "Sparklejollytwinklejingley" from *Elf* saw lyricist Chad Beguelin take Polonius's famous line and turn it into "To thine own elf be true."

465A. That signage for *Goodtime Charley* was on the Palace Theatre marquee between February 20, 1975, and May 31, 1975 (give or take a week or two), during which time filming took place for Neil Simon's *The Sunshine Boys.*

The film garnered an Oscar for George Burns.

466A. Coleman and Fields wrote the song for *Eleanor,* as in Roosevelt. She must have been a bad subject for a musical, if the mythical musical by the same name that's a focal point of *The Prom* is any indication.

467A. The want songs are 1) "I Want to Be Seen with You," 2) "I Want You, Baby," 3) "I Want It All," 4) "I Want to Go to Hollywood," 5) "I Want a Hot Dog for My Roll," and 6) "I Want a Love I Can See."

468A. *Passion,* the musical by Stephen Sondheim and James Lapine, received ten Tony nominations on May 15, 1994—eleven years after Peter Nichols's drama *Passion* had premiered at the Longacre on May 15, 1983.

469A. Lois Lane was not only a character in *Kiss Me, Kate,* but also, more understandably, in *"It's a Bird . . . It's a Plane . . . It's Superman."*

Lisa Kirk played her in the former musical, and Tony-nominated Patricia Marand in the latter.

470A. The 2010 musical *American Idiot* played the St. James Theatre, where its song "St. Jimmy" was heard for 422 performances.

471A. All were songs that were written for other musicals.

1) "It's Today" (*Mame*) was written as "There's No Tune Like a Show Tune" in *Parade*.

2) "Poor Everybody Else" (*Seesaw*), was written for *Sweet Charity*.

3) "Say a Prayer for Me Tonight" (*Gigi*), was written for *My Fair Lady*.

4) "Something Was Missing" (*Annie*), was written as "You Rat You" from the film *The Night They Raided Minsky's*.

5) "You'll Never Get Away from Me" (*Gypsy*) was written as "I'm in Pursuit of Happiness" from the TV musical *Ruggles of Red Gap*.

472A. Alan Jay Lerner in 1976 saw Ken Howard (*Child's Play*) and Patricia Routledge (*Darling of the Day*) billed above the title in his seven-performance *1600 Pennsylvania Avenue*.

In addition, in 1983, his one-performance *Dance a Little Closer* had Len Cariou (*Sweeney Todd*) and George Rose (*My Fair Lady*) billed above the name of the musical that ran all of one performance.

473A. All of the plays were adapted into operas.

1) *Regina* by Marc Blitzstein, 2) *A Streetcar Named Desire* by Andre Previn and Philip Littell, 3) *Our Town* by Ned Rorem and J. D. McClatchy, 4) *Otello* by Giuseppe Verdi and Arrigo Boito, and 5) *A Midsummer Night's Dream* by Benjamin Britten and Peter Pears.

474A. Ben Franklin asks Madame La Comtesse Diane de Vobrillac to marry him. She's astonished and asks "Franklin! You *mean* that?!" to which he responds "I do. I do indeed."

I Do! I Do! was indeed the next musical Robert Preston did on Broadway.

475A. The 2014 film of Sondheim's *Into the Woods* includes "The Sun Won't Set" from Sondheim's *A Little Night Music* as background music when the Prince is giving a ball.

476A. Each show opened at a theater that no longer exists.

1) Ziegfeld, 2) Helen Hayes, 3) Morosco, 4) Century, 5) 54th Street, 6) Bijou, and 7) Playhouse.

477A. Carole Bayer wrote the lyrics for the 1970 musical flop *Georgy*.

In 1979, in conjunction with *innamorato* Marvin Hamlisch, she was lyricist Carole Bayer Sager for their *They're Playing Our Song*.

478A. The film is *Neptune's Daughter*, which is mentioned in composer Galt (*Hair*) MacDermot and lyricist William Dumaresq's song "I Can Carry a Tune" in their 1984 musical *The Human Comedy*.

479A. Jim Morgan heads the York Theatre Company, which does both new musicals and vintage ones.

Jim Morgan is also the name of the scientist who sought Lois Lane's hand in *"It's A Bird . . . It's A Plane . . . It's Superman."*

480A. On the original cast albums of each, you can hear the songwriter at some point in the song.

1) Composer Harold Arlen actually sang the last note of the song when Diahann Carroll couldn't manage it, 2) Sondheim recorded "You ain't gettin' 88 cents from me, Rose," 3) Timothy Gray, who collaborated with Hugh Martin on the score, sang "Forever and a Day," 4) Mel Brooks contributed his voice to "Don't be stupid! Be a smarty! Come and join the Nazi party!"

481A. In *Do I Hear a Waltz?* the song "No Understand" has Giovanna, a maid at a Venice pensione, do so poorly in learning English that her employer tells her to study that night and "no see Alfredo."

482A. Meg Boyd tells us in "Six Months out of Every Year"—the opening number of the Tony-winning *Damn Yankees*—that she and Joe met in November 1938, and in December of that year, she agreed to marry him.

Given that *Damn Yankees* opened in 1955, the Boyds have been together at least seventeen years, for the script tells us that "the action takes place some time in the future."

483A. Along with six other states, New York experienced a blackout that plunged the city into darkness. It postponed Harold Rome's play with music by a day.

This was one of the days on which *Fly by Night* took place. Its most arresting scene involved a man who planned to electrocute himself by standing in a filled bathtub and throwing a plugged-in record player into it.

And as he did, the power failed and he survived.

484A. Dick Shawn replaced Tony-winning Zero Mostel in *A Funny Thing Happened on the Way to the Forum* and then Jack (*She Loves Me*) Cassidy in *Fade Out–Fade In*.

He portrayed Lorenzo St. DuBois and sang "Love Power" in the 1968 film *The Producers*. Neither his character nor his song was included in the 2001 stage musical.

485A. Those were the numbers performed on the very first nationally televised Tony Awards on March, 26, 1967, courtesy of ABC.

486A. "All about the Green" in the 2006 musical *The Wedding Singer* mentions "Big Spender," a song from the 1966 musical *Sweet Charity*.

487A. Forty percent of the book musicals to which Jerry Herman provided songs were set in France: *Dear World, The Grand Tour, La Cage aux Folles,* and even *Ben Franklin in Paris*, for which he wrote two songs.

488A. Antoine De Saint-Exupery's 1943 novella *The Little Prince* became a musical film in 1974 by *My Fair Lady*'s Alan Jay Lerner and Frederick Loewe. It received poor reviews and grossed less than $1 million.

In 1982, bookwriter Hugh Wheeler, who'd won Tonys for the libretti of *A Little Night Music* and *Sweeney Todd* and for his revisions to *Candide*, teamed with composer Jon Barry and lyricist Don Black, who'd won the Best Song Oscar for "Born Free." Their *The Little Prince and the Aviator* closed after twenty previews and never officially opened.

In 2022, an international version called *The Little Prince* that relied on dancers and acrobats (and had music but no songs) could only manage thirty-two performances.

489A. All named or alluded to famous plays.

1) "I'm playing Hilde in *The Master Builder*," 2) "Me as King Lear," 3) "*The Crucible?* Boy, what a play!" 4) "Unless I am doing *The Miracle Worker*," 5) "Did I get a rose tattoo?," and 6) "My life resembled *The Cherry Orchard*."

490A. *I Had a Ball,* which opened thirty-one months after *Forum,* has a song called "Dr. Freud" that includes the words "fraud," "afraid," "freed," and "fried."

491A. Philip Barry's *The Philadelphia Story* opened on Broadway in 1939, which led to a film version in 1940.

In 1956, it became a film musical as *High Society*. The original title couldn't be used because the locale was moved to Newport, Rhode Island.

For the 1998 Broadway musical, *High Society* remained the title, for Oyster Bay was its locale.

492A. *A Family Affair,* with music by John Kander, starred Shelley Berman, Eileen Heckart, and Morris Carnovsky to only slightly better advantage than closing out of town.

493A. Not only did each of those Tony-winners have a shorter run than a musical it had bested, but each of them was never filmed, while one of the musicals it had bested did come before the cameras.

    1) *Flower Drum Song,* 2) *Grease,* 3) *Beauty and the Beast,* 4) *Mamma Mia!,* and 5) *Rock of Ages.*

494A. The 2008 Broadway musical called *[title of show]* mentioned a number of Broadway flops in its song "Monkeys and Playbills."

495A. You may have inferred that Charles Strouse was composer of three Tony-winning musicals: *Bye Bye Birdie, Applause,* and *Annie.* You might have easily guessed that Robert Lopez, thanks to *Avenue Q* and *The Book of Mormon,* was the two-time Tony-winning composer of those two Best Musical Tony-winners.

    The rest of the question is murderously hard to answer. But in Strouse's *Bring Back Birdie,* we're told that Albert Peterson's mother was a former vaudevillian named Dolores Zepol—but she had changed her name by simply reversing it from Lopez.

496A. Moss Hart directed *My Fair Lady* thirteen years after he'd written the book and had directed *Lady in the Dark.*

    Hence, our mashup is *My Fair Lady in the Dark.*

497A. John Kander and Fred Ebb won a Best Score for the Tony-winning *Kiss of the Spider Woman* in 1993, a dozen years after they'd won a Best Score for the Tony-nominated *Woman of the Year.*

    Hence, our mashup is *Kiss of the Spider Woman of the Year.*

498A. Stephen Sondheim was born on March 22, 1930; Andrew Lloyd Webber was born March 22, 1948.

Sondheim's biggest flop was the 1964 musical *Anyone Can Whistle,* which could only manage nine performances.

That, however, was nine more than the 1996 production of Lloyd Webber's *Whistle Down the Wind* could muster; it closed in Washington.

Hence, our mashup is *Anyone Can Whistle Down the Wind.*

499A.

1) "If I Had a Million Dollars," *$1,000,000*

2) "Five Zeros," *$1,000,000 divided by $200,000 = $5*

3) "Four Black Dragons," *$5 minus $4 = $1*

4) "Two Nobodies in New York," *$1 divided by 2 = $0.50*

5) "Two Ladies," *$0.50 divided by 2 = $0.25*

6) "Ten Duel Commandments," *$0.25 minus .10 = $0.15*

7) "It Takes Two," *$0.15 divided by 2 is $0.075.*

What do you have?

As they sing in *The Pajama Game,* "Seven-and-a-half cents."

Finally

500A. *1776!*